ANTHOLOGY FOR

# The Musician's Guide to Theory and Analysis

SECOND EDITION

ANTHOLOGY FOR

# The Musician's Guide to Theory and Analysis

SECOND EDITION

*Jane Piper Clendinning*

*Elizabeth West Marvin*

W. W. NORTON & COMPANY
NEW YORK • LONDON

Printed in the United States of America
Second Edition

Editor: Maribeth Payne
Associate Editor: Courtney Hirschey
Editorial assistant: Ariella Foss

Production manager: Benjamin Reynolds
Art director: Hope Miller Goodell
Book design by Rubina Yeh and David Botwinik
Page composition and layout: Roberta Flechner
Music typesetting: Music by Design/Willow Graphics
New music scans: Alex Price
Manufacturing by QuadGraphics—Eusey, MA

ISBN: 978-0-393-93134-1

W. W. Norton & Company, Inc., 500 Fifth Avenue, New York, N.Y. 10110
www.wwnorton.com
W. W. Norton & Company Ltd., Castle House, 75/76 Wells Street, London W1T 3QT

2 3 4 5 6 7 8 9 0

# Contents

# Preface

The study of music theory is at its very heart an aural endeavor: its study is all about sounds—how and why music sounds the way it does. For this reason, we strongly believe in approaching theoretical instruction aurally, by listening repeatedly to diverse pieces of music and drawing out their structural principles through that experience. This anthology and its accompanying recordings are designed to accompany our textbook, *The Musician's Guide to Theory and Analysis*, but it can easily be adapted for use with any number of music theory texts that cover harmony, counterpoint, and form in tonal and post-tonal music. Our text's approach to learning music theory is a "spiral" one, in which we revisit the anthology's core repertoire from chapter to chapter as we introduce new concepts—a single piece might be used first to illustrate scales, then be revisited to study its triads, cadence types, secondary dominants, common-chord modulation, sequence, and binary form. We hope that by listening to these works often you will get to know the compositions in the Anthology well—until you can hear each one in your head, the same way you can hear familiar songs just by thinking about them.

Why purchase an anthology in an era of free public-domain scores and easy internet downloads? We believe that providing all these scores together in one place is a service that will save you time and effort, and taken together with the coordinated recordings—one recording (and sometimes two) for every single work in the anthology—the package of scores and recordings costs far less than the $.99 per track that popular download sites charge. More than that, we have taken considerable care in selecting music that we like, that many of our students have performed, and that they (and we) have enjoyed exploring together. Some of the works should be familiar to you ("Greensleeves," "The Stars and Stripes Forever"), while others will probably be new. Some are classics of the repertoire: Mozart and Beethoven piano sonata movements, German Lieder from Schubert and Schumann song cycles, and groundbreaking compositions by Penderecki and Reich. There are pieces for varied performing ensembles that span many contrasting musical styles.

In the second edition, we have worked to incorporate the ideas of helpful reviewers while retaining the key features of the first edition. Among the biggest changes is the size of the collection, which includes approximately forty new works: we have added more chorales and hymns, contrapuntal works, and pieces representing nineteenth-century chromaticism and impressionism. This edition also features a new chronological index and short headnotes for each score, placing the works into historical context, as well as new translations by the authors that allow closer word-by-word comparison with the original texts.

## Highlights:

**Over 100 works** or movements are represented, including:

- 26 twentieth-century compositions, ranging from pre-1950 (Gershwin, Stravinsky, Bartók, Schoenberg, Webern) to post-1950 (Penderecki, Reich, Corigliano, Tavener)
- Arias and art songs with literal, word-by-word translations by the authors to assist in analysis of text painting
- Music by women and African American composers (Clara Schumann, Hensel, Joplin)
- Music in popular genres (ragtime and Broadway songs by Gershwin and Willson)
- Music for band, wind ensemble, and orchestra (Chance, Sousa, Penderecki)
- Music for choir (Bach, Tavener, Handel, Mozart)
- Music featuring solo instruments (flute, clarinet, trumpet, guitar, violin)
- Keyboard performances on piano, fortepiano, harpsichord, and organ

**DVDs:** Every work in the anthology is recorded on DVD, in high-quality professional performances by faculty and graduate students from the Eastman School of Music. The recordings are in mp3 format: listen on your computer or rip them to your iPod or other mp3 player for portability.

**Comparison performances:** Several works are given in two contrasting performances for comparison and discussion in class. These contrasting interpretations demonstrate performance-practice issues such as ornamentation, or contrast historical instruments and tunings with modern ones (Mozart, Purcell, Joplin). Bach chorales are recorded in three formats for analysis and discussion in class: choral performance, soprano-bass frameworks on organ, and full SATB texture on organ. Hymn tunes are similarly recorded in soprano-bass and SATB formats.

## Our Thanks to . . .

A work of this size and scope is helped along the way by many people. We are especially grateful for the support of our families—Elizabeth A. Clendinning and Jeffrey L. Armstrong; and Glenn, Russell, and Caroline West. Our work together as co-authors has been incredibly rewarding, and we are thankful for that collaboration and friendship. We also thank Joel Phillips (Westminster Choir College) for his many important contributions—pedagogical, musical, and personal—to our project, and especially for the coordinated aural skills component of this package: *The Musician's Guide to Aural Skills,* now co-authored with Paul Murphy (State University of New York at Fredonia). While working on the project, we have received encouragement and useful ideas from our many colleagues and students at Florida State University and the Eastman School of Music as well as from music theory teachers across the country. We thank them all for their willingness to share their years of experience with us.

For subvention of the recordings that accompany the text and anthology, and for his continued support of strong music theory pedagogy, we thank Douglas Lowry (Dean of the Eastman School of Music). For production of all recordings, our thanks go to recording engineers Mike Farrington and John Ebert, who worked tirelessly with Elizabeth Marvin on recording and editing sessions, as well as to Helen Smith, who oversees Eastman's Office of Technology and Music Production. We also acknowledge the strong contributions of David Peter Coppen, archivist of the Eastman Audio Archive, for his work contacting faculty and alumni for permission to include their performances among our recordings. We finally thank the faculty and students of the Eastman School who gave so generously of their time to make these recordings. The joy of their music making contributed mightily to this project.

We are indebted to the Norton staff for their commitment to *The Musician's Guide* and their painstaking care in producing these volumes. Most notable among these are Maribeth Payne, Susan Gaustad, and Steve Hoge, whose contributions are based on their love for music and understanding of music theory, as well their considerable knowledge of editing and publishing. Justin Hoffman was invaluable in preparing the headnotes, compiling the timeline of works, checking scores and editions, assisting with coordination of the recording sessions, and attending to many details in the preparation of this Anthology. Michael Ochs's help with the German translations was greatly appreciated. Finally, we thank Courtney Hirschey, Ariella Foss, and Nancy Rodwan for their diligent pursuit of copyright permissions, careful attention to containing costs while providing the best selection of scores and recorded music possible, and for their oversight of the production aspects of this multifaceted project through to completion. Our sincere and ongoing gratitude to one and all.

*Jane Piper Clendinning*
*Elizabeth West Marvin*

**Anonymous**

Minuet in D Minor, from the *Anna Magdalena Bach Notebook*

This minuet, by an unknown composer, is part of a collection of short keyboard compositions by Johann Sebastian Bach and others. The collection appears in a notebook that Bach gave to his second wife, Anna Magdalena, in 1725. In the early eighteenth century, such notebooks were useful tools for teaching performance and composition, and Bach assembled several for his family.

## Johann Sebastian Bach (1685–1750)

From Cantata No. 140, "Wachet auf": "Er kommt" (recitative)

Bach wrote the cantata "Wachet auf" in 1731 for performance in the Thomaskirche, a church in Leipzig where he served as Kapellmeister (music director). Most of Bach's cantatas are choral-vocal compositions for performance in Lutheran churches. The texts of such cantatas expound upon the religious themes of the particular day for which it was written. Cantatas frequently include polyphonic choral movements, arias for soloists, and chorale settings. The text on which this cantata is based, relating the parable of the ten virgins, is assigned to the twenty-seventh Sunday after Trinity, which occurs in the church year only when Easter comes very early. Because of the infrequency of this date in the liturgical calendar, it is one of the few Bach cantatas whose date of composition is definitively known.

### No. 2. Recitative

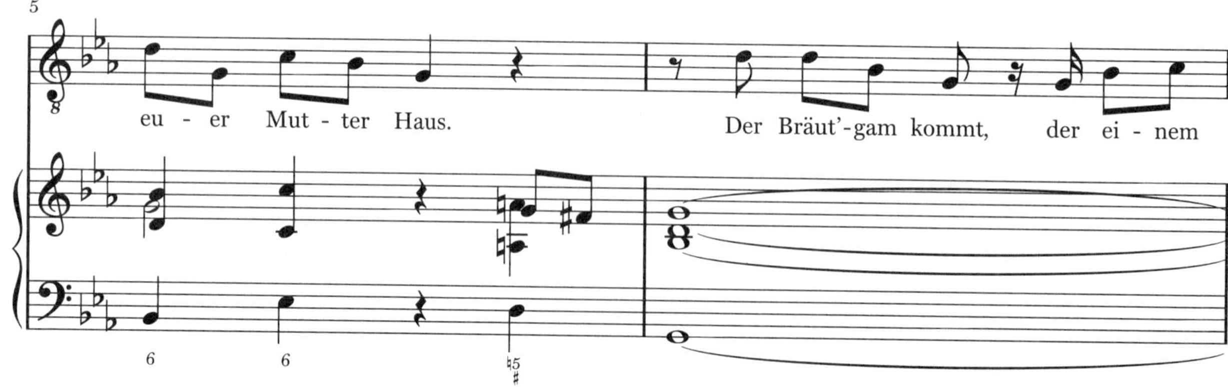

7
Re - he und jun - gen Hir - sche gleich auf de - nen Hü - geln springt und euch das
9
Mahl der Hoch - zeit bringt. Wacht auf, er-mun-tert euch! den
11
Bräut'-gam zu em-pfan-gen; dort! se-het, kommt er her-ge - gan-gen!

## TEXT AND TRANSLATION

"Er kommt"

Er kommt, er kommt,
Der Bräut'gam kommt!
Ihr Töchter Zions, kommt heraus,
Sein Ausgang eilet aus der Höhe
In euer Mutter Haus.
Der Bräut'gam kommt, der einen Rehe
Und jungen Hirsche gleich
Auf denen Hügeln springt
Und euch das Mahl der Hochzeit bringt.
Wacht auf, ermuntert euch!
Den Bräut'gam zu empfangen;
Dort! sehet, kommt er hergegangen!

"He comes"

He comes, he comes,
The bridegroom comes!
Zion's daughters, come out,
Hasten his exit from the heights
To your mother's house.
The bridegroom comes, who like a deer
And young stag
Springs from the hills,
To bring you the wedding feast.
Wake up, be encouraged
To welcome the bridegroom.
There! Behold, he comes this way!

## Johann Sebastian Bach

From Cantata No. 208 ("The Hunt"): "Soll denn der Pales Opfer" (recitative) and "Schafe können sicher weiden" (aria)

Bach's Hunt Cantata, a secular work, was first performed in 1713 for the birthday of Prince Christian of Saxon-Weißenfels. The libretto, which borrows from Greek mythology, was written by the German poet Salomo Franck, whose texts appear in dozens of Bach's cantatas. Although the cantata as a whole is not frequently performed today, this aria has become well known on its own, and its imagery of the shepherd watching over the flock has been adapted from its secular origins to sacred uses.

Libretto by Salomo Franck

8
Held, zur Freud'
und Lust be - we-gen!
Andante con moto
Treble Recorder 1
Treble Recorder 2
Soprano
Continuo
p
p
4
f
p
f
p
tr
Scha - fe kön - nen si - cher wei - den,

7
wo - ein gu - ter Hir - te wacht, Scha - fe kön - nen si - cher wei - den,
11
Scha - fe kön - nen si - cher wei - den, wo - ein gu - ter
14
Hir - te wacht, wo - ein gu - ter Hir - te

17
wacht.
20
Fine
Wo Re - gen - ten wohl re - gie - ren
Fine
23
kann man Ruh' und Frie - den spü - ren, und was Län - der glück - lich macht,

27
30
Wo Re - gen - ten wohl re - gie - ren, kann man
33
Ruh' und Frie - den spü - ren, Ruh' und Frie -

36
den, Ruh' und Frie - den spü - ren,
39
D. 𝄋 al Fine
und was Län - der glück - lich macht. Scha - fe kön - nen,
D. 𝄋 al Fine

## TEXT AND TRANSLATION

| | |
|---|---|
| Soll denn der Pales Opfer hier das letzte sein? Nein! Nein! | So, shall Pales'offering here be the last? No, no! |
| Ich will die Pflicht auch niederlegen,<br>Und da das ganze Land vom Vivat schallt, | I want also to set aside my duty,<br>And since the whole land with "Vivat" [Latin: May he live!] echoes— |
| Auch dieses schöne Feld<br>Zu Ehren unserm Sachsenheld<br>Zur Freud' und Lust bewegen! | Even this beautiful field—<br>To honor our Saxon hero,<br>To stir to joy and passion. |
| Schafe können sicher weiden,<br>Wo ein guter Hirte wacht.<br>Wo Regenten wohl regieren,<br>Kann man Ruh' und Friede spüren<br>Und was Länder glücklich macht. | Sheep may safely graze<br>Where a good shepherd keeps watch.<br>Where rulers rule well,<br>One can feel peace and tranquility,<br>And that which makes countries fortunate. |

## Johann Sebastian Bach

Chaconne, from Violin Partita No. 2 in D Minor

In 1720, Bach completed a set of six compositions for unaccompanied violin, including three partitas (or suites of dance movements). This Chaconne, which concludes the second partita, is longer than the rest of the composition's movements put together. While posing significant challenges for violinists, it remains a remarkable example of a polyphonic form set for a solo instrument.

From *Johann Sebastian Bach: Works for Violin: The Complete Sonatas and Partitas for Unaccompanied Violin; The Six Sonatas for Violin and Clavier.* New York: Dover Publications, Inc.

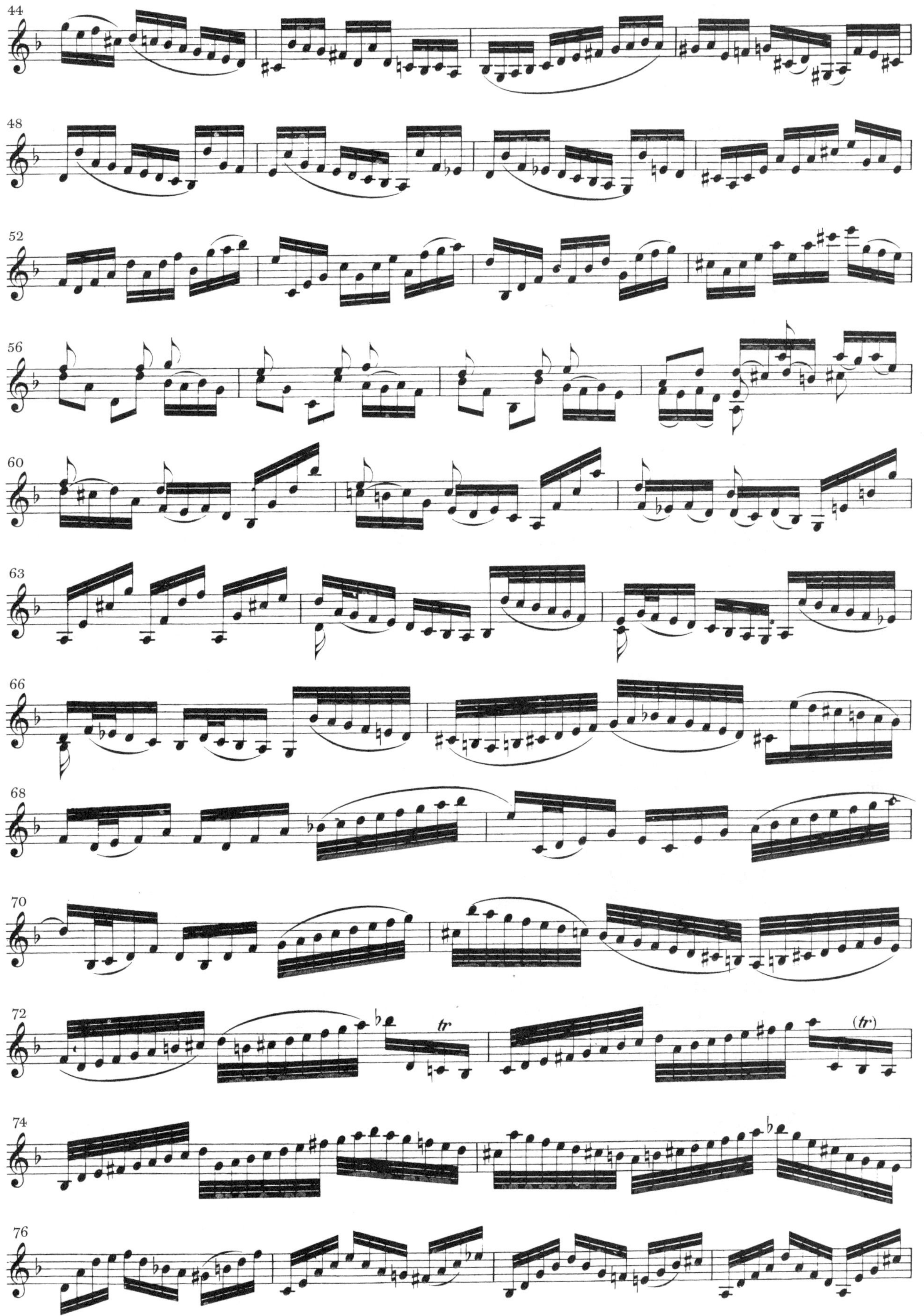
44
48
52
56
60
63
66
68
70
72
tr
(tr)
74
76

80
84
86
88
arpeggio
95
103
111
118
122
125

132
136
143
148
152
156
160
164
167
170
173

176
181
186
191
197
arpeggio
203
208
212
215
218
221

224
227
230
233
236
239
241
243
245
247
251

## Johann Sebastian Bach

Chorales

"Aus meines Herzens Grunde" (No. 1)

The German Lutheran chorale tradition featured congregational singing of familiar melodies that were harmonized by many composers of the era. These tunes were well known to audiences of the time, and were also featured in variation sets, organ chorale preludes, and as movements of larger choral works. "Aus meines Herzens Grunde" is the first chorale in the collection of 317 of J. S. Bach's chorale harmonizations edited by his son, C. P. E. Bach, first published in four volumes between 1784 and 1787.

Aus mei - nes Her - zens Grun - de sag' ich dir
in die - ser Mor - gen - stun - de dar - zu mein
6
Lob und Dank, o Gott in dei - nem Thron, dir
Le - be - lang,
11
zu Lob, Preis und Eh - ren, durch Chri - stum,
16
un - sern Her - ren, dein' ein - ge - bor - nen Sohn.

# "O Haupt voll Blut und Wunden" (No. 74)

This chorale appears repeatedly in the *St. Matthew Passion*, a musical retelling of the story of the crucifixion, each time with a different text and harmonization. Bach composed the passion in 1727 for performance in the Thomaskirche. This chorale, in one of Bach's harmonizations, is still sung in Protestant churches today in the season of Lent, preceding Easter.

# "Wachet auf" (No. 179)

"Wachet auf" appears in several movements of Bach's Cantata No. 140 (1731) of the same name: as the theme for a polyphonic choral movement, as the cantus firmus for a ritornello-based movement, and as a four-part chorale. This harmonization is the last movement of the cantata. Another movement from this cantata is the recitative "Er kommt" (p. 2), and the chorale prelude (p. 23) is a transcription for organ of the ritornello-based movement.

17
Wohl - auf, der Bräut' - gam kommt,
21
Steht auf, die Lamp - en nehmt!
25
Hal - le - lu - jah! Macht
29
euch be - reit zu der Hoch - zeit, Ihr
33
müss - et ihm ent - ge - gen geh'n.

## TEXTS AND TRANSLATIONS

"Aus meines Herzens Grunde"

Aus meines Herzens Grunde
Sag' ich dir Lob und Dank,
In dieser Morgenstunde
Darzu mein Lebelang,
O Gott in deinem Thron,
Dir zu Lob, Preis und Ehren,
Durch Christum, unsern Herren,
Dein' eingebornen Sohn.

"From my heart's foundation"

From my heart's foundation
I offer you praise and thanks,
In this morning hour,
Through my whole life long.
O God on your throne,
To you praise, exaltation, and honor,
Through Christ, our Lord,
Your only begotten son.

"O Haupt voll Blut und Wunden"

O Haupt voll Blut und Wunden
Voll Schmerz und voller Hohn,
O Haupt, zu Spott gebunden
Mit einer Dornenkron,
O Haupt, sonst schön gezieret
Mit höchster Ehr und Zier
Jetzt aber hoch schimpfieret,
Gegrüsset seist du mir!

"O head, full of blood and wounds"

O head, full of blood and wounds,
Full of sorrow and full of scorn,
O head, to mockery bound
With a crown of thorns,
O head, once beautifully adorned
With highest honor and renown,
But now highly insulted,
Let me salute you!

"Wachet auf"

Wachet auf, ruft uns die Stimme,
Der Wächter sehr hoch auf der Zinne:
Wach auf, du Stadt Jerusalem!

Mitternacht heißt diese Stunde,
Sie rufen uns mit hellem Munde:
Wo seid ihr klugen Jungfrauen?

Wohl auf, der Bräut'gam kommt,
Steht auf, die Lampen nehmt!
Halleluia!

Macht euch bereit
Zu der Hochzeit,
Ihr müsset ihm entgegen geh'n.

"Wake up!"

Wake up! the voice calls to us,
The watchman very high on the walls calls,
Wake up, city of Jerusalem!

Midnight this hour is called,
They call us with bright voices,
Where are you, clever young women?

Wake up, the bridegroom comes,
Stand up, take up the lamps!
Halleluia!

Make yourselves ready
For the wedding.
You must go out to meet him.

## Johann Sebastian Bach

Chorale Prelude on "Wachet auf" (Schübler chorale)

This prelude is part of a collection of six chorale preludes (contrapuntal embellishments of chorale tunes) by Bach that were engraved and published by Johann Georg Schübler and appeared in the late 1740s. Based on the chorale "Wachet auf" (p. 20), the piece is an organ transcription of a movement from the cantata of the same name. The chorale tune appears, in a relatively unadorned form, beginning in measure 13 in the organist's left hand.

From *Johann Sebastian Bach: Organ Music.* New York: Dover Publications, Inc.

20
1.
2.
tr
25
29
33

37
tr
41
tr
tr
tr
44
tr
48
tr
tr
tr

52
tr

## Johann Sebastian Bach

Inventions

Around 1720, Bach composed a number of two-voice contrapuntal keyboard works, called inventions, for his ten-year-old son, Wilhelm Friedemann; these include the Inventions in D Minor and F Major. Bach's inventions were intended to teach students how to play two simultaneous lines on the harpsichord and how to develop a musical idea in the course of a piece.

### Invention in D Minor

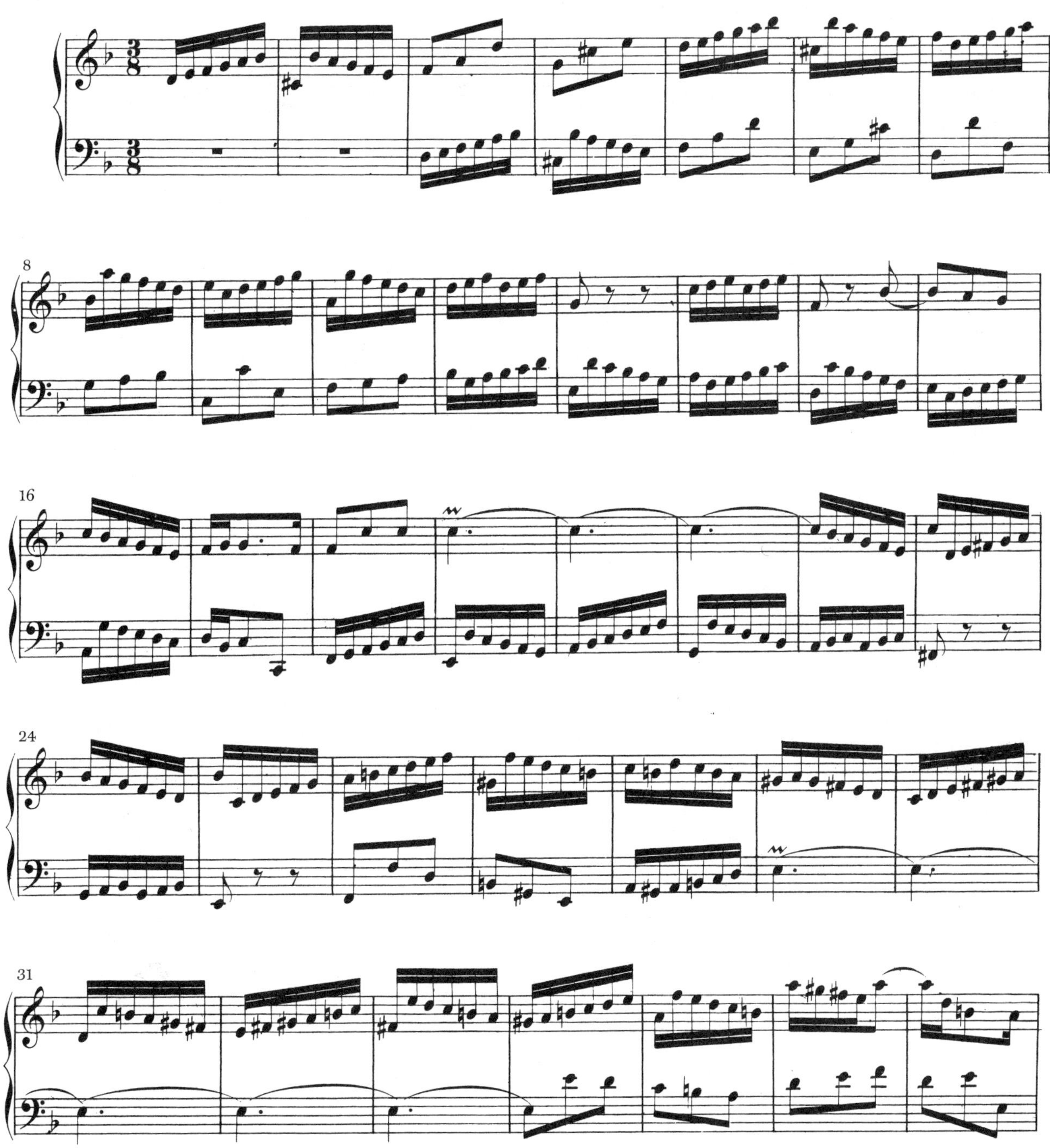


From *Johann Sebastian Bach: Keyboard Music.* New York: Dover Publications, Inc.

38
45

# Invention in F Major

15
17
19
21
23
25

27
29
32

## Johann Sebastian Bach

### Fugue in E♭ Major for organ (*St. Anne*), from *Clavierübung* III

The "St. Anne" Fugue, written in 1739, is one of Bach's most monumental and famous organ compositions. The name, which did not originate with Bach, refers to the initial melody's resemblance to the hymn tune "St. Anne" (p. 220). The Prelude and Fugue in E♭ Major are the opening and closing works to Bach's *Clavierübung,* Part III (the Prelude at the beginning and the Fugue at the end), which also includes twenty-one chorale preludes and four duets. The "St. Anne" Fugue has three distinct sections and three fugue subjects, two of which are combined at its climax.

From *Johann Sebastian Bach: Organ Music.* New York: Dover Publications, Inc.

21
26
31
36
40

44
48
52
56
60

64
68
72
76
80
12
8

83
86
89
91
94

96
99
101
103
105

109
111
113
115

## Johann Sebastian Bach

Passacaglia in C Minor for organ

Bach, who was better known during his lifetime as an organist than as a composer, wrote and performed the Passacaglia in C Minor between 1708 and 1712, when he was serving as organist at the St. Blasius Church in Mühlhausen. A passacaglia, a common genre of baroque keyboard music, consists of a series of variations over a repeated bass line. This famous passacaglia concludes with a double fugue (not given here) that is based on the same theme.

From *Johann Sebastian Bach: Toccatas, Fantasias, Passacaglia and Other Works for Organ.* New York: Dover Publications, Inc.

33
38
43
48
52

56
61
65
69
73

78
83
87
92
97

101
105
110
115
120

124
129
133
3
3
3
137
3
3
140

143
148
154
159
164

**Johann Sebastian Bach**

Prelude, from Cello Suite No. 2 in D Minor

This prelude is the first movement of a suite of dance pieces for solo cello, composed by Bach around 1720 when he was serving as the director of court music at Cöthen. During his years there, Bach focused his energies on secular instrumental music, and the Cello Suite No. 2 is one of six suites for solo cello dating from the period.

From *Johann Sebastian Bach: Complete Suites for Unaccompanied Cello and Sonatas for Viola da Gamba*. New York: Dover Publications, Inc.

41
45
49
52
56

## Johann Sebastian Bach

From *The Well-Tempered Clavier,* Book I

*The Well-Tempered Clavier* consists of two books, published by Bach in 1722 and 1742, each containing twenty-four paired preludes and fugues, one pair in each major and minor key. "Well-tempered" refers to tuning; a well-tempered keyboard instrument is tuned such that it can be played in any key. A number of earlier tuning systems, or "temperaments," based on the pure tuning of particular intervals, were in use during Bach's life; in these temperaments, keys close to C major sounded pleasing, but modulation to distant keys introduced out-of-tune intervals. Only later, with acceptance of equal temperament, could all twenty-four keys be used equally.

### Prelude in C Major

From *Johann Sebastian Bach: The Well-Tempered Clavier, Books I and II, Complete*. New York: Dover Publications, Inc.

20
24
28
32

# Prelude in C Minor

19
22
25
28
Presto
31
34
Adagio
Allegro
36

# Fugue in C Minor

16
19
22
25
28

# Fugue in D♯ Minor

45
51
58
64
70
76
82

# Fugue in G Minor

18
21
24
26
29
32

## Samuel Barber (1910–1981)

"Sea-Snatch," from *Hermit Songs*

Samuel Barber wrote the song cycle *Hermit Songs* in 1952–53. The cycle's texts come from anonymous (and somewhat scandalous) poetry written in the margins of medieval manuscripts by monks. The work was premiered in 1953 at the Library of Congress by soprano Leontyne Price, with the composer at the piano.

9
King - dom of Heav - en;
f
sf
Ped. Ped. Ped. Ped.
13
the wind has con - sumed us, swal-lowed us, as tim-ber is de -
Ped.
17
voured by crim - son fire from Heav - en.
più f
marcato

20
24
mf
p
It has bro-ken us, it has crushed us, it has drowned us, O
cresc. molto
sf
p
sf
cresc. molto
Ped.
28
ff
King of the star-bright King-dom of Heav-en!
ff
Ped.

## Béla Bartók (1881–1945)

*Bagatelle,* Op. 6, No. 2

The *Bagatelles* are short piano pieces that Bartók composed in 1908. In these early works, Bartók explores many techniques that will become important to his later compositions, including ostinatos, changing meters (both seen here), and borrowed folk melodies.

13
dim.
16
p
3/2
2/2
sf
dim.
p
19
p
22
sempre p
26

## Béla Bartók

From *Mikrokosmos*

"Bulgarian Rhythm" and "From the Island of Bali" both appear in *Mikrokosmos,* a six-volume series for beginning to advanced pianists. These books were begun for Bartók's son Péter's piano instruction; published in 1940, they reflect Bartók's life-long interest in musical pedagogy. The works also form a compendium of the composer's compositional techniques, including asymmetrical and changing meters, unconventional key signatures and modal materials, use of Bulgarian and other folk materials, symmetrical musical structures, and rhythmic ostinati.

### "Bulgarian Rhythm" (No. 115)

18

*cresc.*

21

*mf*

*mf*

25

*cresc.*

"From the Isle of Bali" (No. 109)

22
ff

26
poco allarg.
sf
(prol. Ped.)

Andante
31
p, dolce
m.s.
dim.

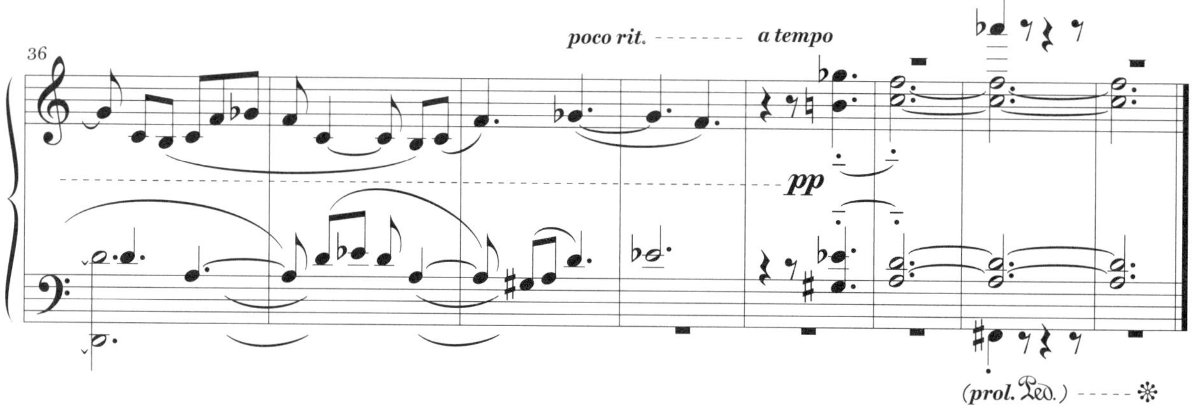
36
poco rit.
a tempo
pp
(prol. Ped.)

## Béla Bartók

"Song of the Harvest," for two violins

The "Song of the Harvest" appears in a set of forty-four violin duets that Bartók assembled for the German violin teacher Erich Dofein. Like the *Mikrokosmos,* these duets are arranged in a pedagogical sequence from simplest to most difficult. They borrow from and imitate features of a number of Eastern European folk repertoires.

21
Tempo II.
poco a poco allarg.
f
f
28
Tempo I.
rallentando
p
p
pp

## Ludwig van Beethoven (1770–1827)

*Für Elise*

This short work, one of Beethoven's most popular keyboard pieces, was not published until after his death. It is also known as the *Bagatelle* No. 25 in A Minor (cataloged as a work without opus number, WoO 59). Although there is much speculation, no one knows exactly who Elise was.

From *Ludwig van Beethoven: Complete Bagatelles for Piano*. New York: Dover Publications, Inc.

34
38
43
49
55
61

67
73
78
3
3
3
pp
8
82
87
93

99

## Ludwig van Beethoven

Piano Sonata in C Minor, Op. 13 (*Pathétique*), second and third movements

Beethoven composed the *Pathétique* Sonata in 1799, at age twenty-seven, during his first decade composing and performing in Vienna. The subtitle, *Pathétique,* which would have appealed to nineteenth-century audiences, means "with pathos." The work was dedicated to Prince Karl von Lichnowsky, who was a supporter and patron to both Mozart and Beethoven. In the recordings that accompany this anthology, the second movement is performed on fortepiano, an early keyboard from Beethoven's era. The third movement, for comparison, is played on a modern piano.

From *Ludwig van Beethoven: Complete Piano Sonatas, Volume I.* New York: Dover Publications, Inc.

19
23
cresc.
(p)
cresc.
p
p
28
pp
p
33
37
pp
40
cresc.
sf
sf

43
*sf*
*decresc.*
*fp*
*pp*
46
48
*cresc.*
51
*p*
55
58

61
64
*pp*
67
70
*rinf.*
*rinf.*
*rinf.*
*pp*
*pp*

RONDO.
Allegro.
p
6
11
cresc.
16
tr
f
fp
fp
24
dolce
29
cresc.
p
sf

34
cresc.
38
42
cresc.
50
54
cresc.
57

62
66
70
cresc.
74
tr
f
p
79
p
89

98
cresc.
103
f
sf
cresc.
108
ff
112
sf
sf
sf
116
ff
sf
p
122

127
132
*sf*
*p dolce*
137
*cresc.*
143
147
151
*p*

157
165
calando
p
172
177
cresc.
182
p
cresc.
sf
sf
ff
187
sf
sf
p
cresc.

191
sf
f
sf
195
sf
ff
200
sf
p
decresc.
205
pp
ff

## Ludwig van Beethoven

Piano Sonata in C Major, Op. 53 (*Waldstein*), first movement

The *Waldstein* Sonata exemplifies the second of the three periods into which historians frequently divide Beethoven's work. The middle period is sometimes known as the "heroic" period, during which Beethoven composed Symphonies 3 through 8 and some of his most famous piano sonatas (including also the *Moonlight* and *Appassionata*). Composed in 1805, this sonata takes its name from Beethoven's friend and supporter Count Ferdinand von Waldstein, to whom it is dedicated.

From *Ludwig van Beethoven: Complete Piano Sonatas, Volume II.* New York: Dover Publications, Inc.

18
pp
21
cresc.
p
24
26
cresc.
f
sf
sf
sf
29
decresc.
decresc.
32
p
dolce e molto legato

37
cresc.
sf
cresc.
p
43
dolce
cresc.
46
sf
p
cresc.
50
54
decresc.
58
cresc.
f
61
ff

64
67
70
73
76
80
85
sf
p
fp
decresc.
pp
cresc.
tr
1.
2.

88
cresc.
pp
pp
93
97
cresc.
f
100
p
cresc.
103
f
pp
106

109
cresc.
3
3
112
f
115
118
121
124

127
130
134
f
p
137
f
p
140
decresc.
pp
143

146
cresc.
3
cresc.
149
3
3
cresc.
1
152
f
sf
sf
155
ff
pp
159
pp
163
cresc.

166
f
sf
sf
decresc.
pp
171
pp
174
f
pp
177
pp
180
cresc.
183
p

186
cresc.
189
f
sf
sf
sf
192
decresc.
p
dolce
198
cresc.
sf
p
cresc.
p
204
dolce
cresc.
207
sf
p
3
cresc.

211
f
215
decresc.
219
cresc.
f
222
ff
225
sf
sf
228
sf
sf
p
fp

231
1) decresc.
pp
cresc.
tr
234
tr
fp
238
fp
242
cresc.
p
cresc.
p
247
cresc.
p
pp
252
f
p
f
sf
sf

256
sf
sf
ff
f
p
260
cresc.
pp
263
pp
266
269
cresc.
272
sf
sf
sf
sf
sf
sf

275
ff
f
277
sf
fp
279
281
sf
sf
p dolce
285
cresc.
sf
p
cresc.
p
cresc.
p
293
a tempo
ri - tar - dan-do
cresc.
p
pp
cresc.

298
ff
sf
ff

## Ludwig van Beethoven

Sonatina in F Major, Op. Posth., second movement

Beethoven composed several sonatinas, or brief sonatas, before making the substantial journey from his birthplace, Bonn, to the cultural capital of the German-speaking world, Vienna. The Sonatina in F, composed between 1790 and 1792, was not published during his lifetime.

From *Beethoven Masterpieces for Solo Piano, 25 Works*. New York: Dover Publications, Inc.

37
45
53
61
70
ad libitum
(a tempo)
p
79
mf
p
86
mf
p
f

## Johannes Brahms (1833–1897)

"Die Mainacht"

Brahms set "Die Mainacht," by the eighteenth-century German poet Ludwig Hölty, in 1866. The text, filled with images of nature, was also set by Franz Schubert and Fanny Hensel.

· Text by Ludwig Christoph Heinrich Hölty

11
wandl'ich trau-rig von Busch zu Busch.
15
Ü-ber-hül-let vom Laub gir-ret ein Tau-ben-paar sein Ent-zük-ken mir
p
cresc.
19
vor; a-ber ich wen-de mich,
f
f
23
su-che dunk-le-re Schat-ten,
p dimin.

27
und die ein - - sa - me Trä - - - -
espressivo
30
- - - ne rinnt.
dimin. ritard.
33
Wann, o lä - chelndes Bild, wel - cheswie Mor - gen - rot
a tempo
36
durch die See - le mir strahlt, find ich auf Er - den dich?

39
Und die ein - - sa - me Trä - - - - -
p cresc. legato
42
- - - ne bebt mir hei - - ßer,
mf
45
hei - - - ßer die Wang her -
p

## TEXT AND TRANSLATION

| "Die Mainacht" | "The May Night" |
|---|---|
| Wann der silberne Mond durch die Gesträuche blinkt,<br>Und sein schlummerndes Licht über den Rasen streut,<br>Und die Nachtigall flötet,<br>Wandl' ich traurig von Busch zu Busch. | When the silvery moon beams through the shrubbery,<br>And its slumbering light scatters over the lawn,<br>And the nightingale flutes,<br>I wander sadly from bush to bush. |
| Überhüllet vom Laub girret ein Taubenpaar<br>Sein Entzücken mir vor; aber ich wende mich,<br>Suche dunklere Schatten,<br>Und die einsame Träne rinnt. | Veiled by leaves, a pair of doves coo<br>Their delight in front of me, but I turn,<br>Seeking darker shadows,<br>And the lonely tear runs down. |
| Wann, o lächelndes Bild, welches wie Morgenrot<br>Durch sie Seele mir strahlt, find ich auf Erden dich?<br>Und die einsame Träne<br>Bebt mir heisser die Wang herab! | When, O smiling image, who shines like rosy dawn<br>Through my soul, shall I find you on earth?<br>And the lonely tear<br>Trembles, burning, down my cheek. |

## Johannes Brahms

Intermezzo in A Major, Op. 118, No. 2

The Intermezzo in A Major, published in 1893, comes from one of four collections of short piano pieces that Brahms compiled during the last decade of his life. The title "Intermezzo" was first used in the Renaissance to describe short musical interludes that separated acts of a play. By the nineteenth century, the term had come to mean a short, lyrical instrumental composition, most often for piano.

From *Johannes Brahms: Complete Shorter Works for Solo Piano*. New York: Dover Publications, Inc.

18
cresc.
23
legato
28
f
espress.
p dim.
33
calando
dolce
38
cresc. un poco animato
43
rit. - - - più lento
p
p

49
in tempo
53
rit.
57
più lento
pp
legato
una corda
rit.
pp
62
rit.
Tempo I
p
espress.
cresc.
tre corde
67
f
71
p rit.
dolce
pp

76
rf
dolce
81
espress.
86
cresc.
91
legato
97
f
espress
p dim.
calando
dolce
103
cresc. un poco animato

109
rit. - - - più lento
p

## Johannes Brahms

*Variations on a Theme by Haydn,* theme (two pianos)

Over the course of his life, Brahms wrote numerous sets of variations on themes by other composers, including Schumann, Handel, and Paganini. The *Variations on a Theme by Haydn,* written in 1873, takes the "St. Anthony" Chorale, once believed to be by Haydn, as its theme. Brahms prepared two versions of the piece: the one for two pianos that appears here and another for orchestra.

From *Brahms: Variationen über ein Thema von Joseph Haydn Opus 56b.* New York: C. F. Peters Corporation. n.d.

11
I
p
pp
p
pp
17
I
f
f
f
24
I
1.
2.
dim. smorzando
p
1.
2.
dim. smorzando
p

## John Barnes Chance (1932–1972)

*Variations on a Korean Folk Song,* excerpts

Chance's *Variations on a Korean Folk Song,* written in 1967, is based on the folk song "Arirang," which Chance first heard while in Korea with an army band. Like all of his compositions, this piece is for wind ensemble. This folk song is still well known in Korea and abroad (it appears, for example, in the 1990 Presbyterian hymnal with English text), and has often served as the theme for variation sets by other composers.

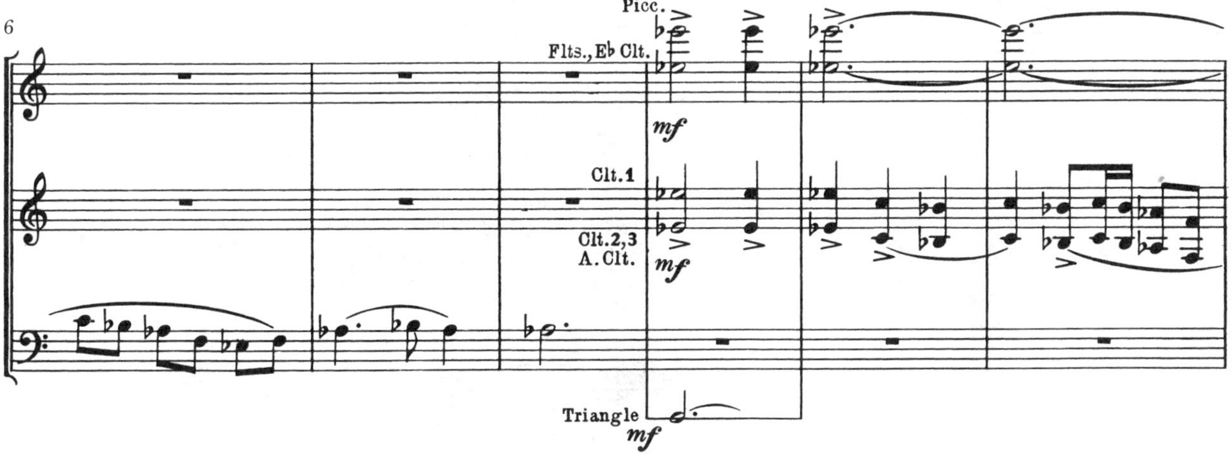

17
-Picc.
p
Bar., A.Sax., T.Sax.
mf cantabile
p
Tbns., Tuba
Lower W.W.
22
Obs.
Clt.1
Clt. 2,3
f
Hns.
-Bar., Sax.
27
poco a poco
p
+Bar., Sax.
f
p
32
rall.
+Picc.
+Tpts.

38
Vivace (♩=132)
Obs., A.Clt., A.Sax.
Bssns., T.Sax.
Temple Blocks
Gong
(With snare stick)
42
Picc. 8va, E♭ Clt.
B♭ Cls., Xylo.
+B. Clt., B. Sax.
Gong
45
- B.Clt., T. Sax.
- B.Sax.
- Bssns.
48
Tpts.
Tbns.
Cymbs.

51
+Hns.
Low. W. W.
Bar., Tuba
Gong
ff
Con Islancio (♩= 144)
199
(♩=♩)
Sn. Dr.
mf
Cymb.
mf (with snare stick on dome)
203
mf
Gong (with snare stick)

207

211

215
E♭ Clt.
Clt. 1

219
Clts., Saxes.

223

Tpts.

*ff sostenuto*

Hns.

Tbns. *ff sostenuto*

231
235
3
3
3

239
tr
3
3
-Clt. 2+3
A. Clt., A. Sax.
W.W.
ff
ff
f
f
245
(tr)

(tr)
250
W.W. ff
Tpts. 2,3
W.W., Hns.
ff
(tr)
257
sfp
ff
sfp
ff
p subito
ff
p subito
ff
ff
ff

## Frédéric Chopin (1810–1849)

Mazurka in F Minor, Op. 68, No. 4

A mazurka is a dance in triple meter that originated in the Mazovia region of Poland and by the nineteenth century had become popular all over Europe. Chopin, who grew up in the Mazovia region, composed numerous mazurkas. This one, sketched in 1846 and published after his death, was one of his last contributions to the genre.

21
tr
mf
Ped.
26
tr
31
pp
sempre legato
36
D.C. dal segno senza fine

## Frédéric Chopin

Nocturne in E♭ Major, Op. 9, No. 2

Chopin included the Nocturne in E♭ Major in a set of nocturnes published in 1832, shortly after he had left his native Poland. A nocturne is a composition intended to invoke the sounds or feeling of the night. Chopin composed numerous nocturnes, consisting of slow, song-like melodies that are accompanied by arpeggiated chords, often simulating a guitar.

From *Frédéric Chopin: Nocturnes and Polonaises.* New York: Dover Publications, Inc.

poco rall.
Tempo I.
fz p
come sopra.
cresc.
p
poco ritard.
f
poco rall.
Tempo I.
fz p

23
25
poco rubato.
sempre pp
dolcissimo
28
con forza.
stretto.
30

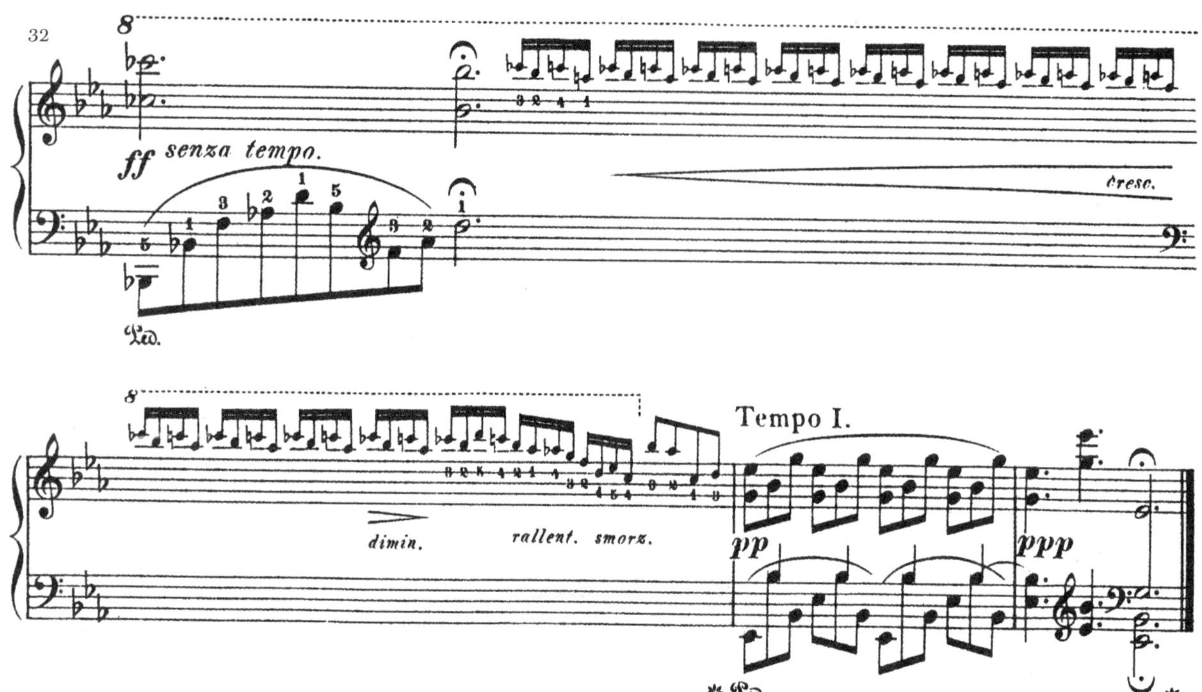
32
8
ff senza tempo.
Ped.
cresc.
dimin.
rallent. smorz.
Tempo I.
pp
ppp
Ped.

**Frédéric Chopin**

Prelude in C Minor, Op. 28, No. 20

This piece is included in a collection of short preludes that Chopin composed in 1839. Like each volume of Bach's *Well-Tempered Clavier* (p. 48), which Chopin was studying when he wrote his own preludes, Op. 28 consists of one prelude in each of the twenty-four major and minor keys. Unlike Bach's, however, Chopin's preludes are not paired with fugues.

From *Frédéric Chopin: Complete Preludes and Etudes.* New York: Dover Publications, Inc.

## Jeremiah Clarke (1674–1707)

*Trumpet Voluntary (Prince of Denmark's March)*

The *Trumpet Voluntary* was likely originally written for solo harpsichord around 1700. It has become famous through the 1878 arrangement for trumpet and organ by Henry Wood. Wood mistakenly believed that the piece was by Henry Purcell, a misattribution that was not corrected until the 1940s.

Arranged by Sue Mitchell Wallace and John H. Head

9
II
ff
Pedal: add II to Ped.
13
17
tr
f
I
f
Pedal: off II

21
tr
Pedal: add II
25
II
ff
29

33
I
Pedal: off II
37
41
II
Pedal: add II to Ped.

45
49
f
I
f
Pedal: off II
53

57
II
ff
Pedal: add II
61
65
II
f
I
Pedal: off II

69
rall.
rall.
Pedal: add Reeds 16', 8', 4'
ff
Maestoso
73
ff
II
ff
77
rit.
rit.

## Muzio Clementi (1752–1832)

Sonatina, Op. 36, No. 1, first movement

Clementi, a renowned piano virtuoso and teacher, composed this sonatina in 1797. It was one of several sonatinas published as a supplement to *Introduction to the Art of Playing on the Piano Forte,* an instructional handbook for pianists. Even today, this work serves a pedagogical role in piano instruction, as it is reprinted in a number of collections of short works for study by intermediate-level pianists.

From *Muzio Clementi: Complete Sonatinas for Piano, Opp. 36, 37, and 38.* New York: Dover Publications, Inc.

16
p
20
f
24
p
28
cresc.
f
32
35

## **Archangelo Corelli (1653–1713)**

Allemanda, from Trio Sonata in A Minor, Op. 4, No. 5

This Allemanda comes from a trio sonata for two violins and continuo instruments, written in 1694 by the Italian composer Archangelo Corelli. *Sonatas de camera* (secular chamber sonatas, as opposed to church sonatas), like Corelli's Op. 4, No. 5, consisted of a series of dance movements. A blank staff is added to the score here for practice writing a continuo realization.

9
p
f
13
17

21
9 6 5 4 6 6 5 5 6 5 7 7 7 7 7 ♯ 9 6

25
p
p
p
9 6 7 ♯ 5 6 5 ♯ 6 9 6 7 ♯ 5 6 5 ♯

## Archangelo Corelli

Preludio, from Sonata in D Minor, Op. 4, No. 8

This Preludio is the first movement of a trio sonata composed in 1694. Despite its name, a trio sonata requires four players for a performance: two soloists (in this case, violinists), a third performer to play the bass line, and a fourth to fill out the harmonies by realizing the figured bass (on an instrument such as the harpsichord).

29
f
p
f
9 8
7
♯
5
6
5
6
4
4
♯
6
6
6
♯
6
♯
6
♯

## John Corigliano (b. 1938)

"Come now, my darling," from *The Ghosts of Versailles*

*The Ghosts of Versailles* received its premiere in 1991 at the Metropolitan Opera in New York. Its plot revolves around an opera-within-an-opera, staged by the French playwright Pierre Beaumarchais for the ghosts of the French court of Louis XVI and Marie Antoinette. The characters who sing this duet, the Countess Rosina and Cherubino, also figure prominently in Mozart's opera *The Marriage of Figaro* (p. 230).

Libretto by William M. Hoffman

10
S
M-s
pp
p
I'm not a - quaint-ed with these parts.
We're in the Gar - den of Earth - ly De-lights.
(p)
14
I'm lost in this land and fright-ened.
To the north is the Vil-lage of Shy
19
mp
My soul is closed to sweet pleas-ures.
Glan - ces.
To the east

23
S
M-s
mp
mf
Rage, bit-ter-ness, and hate con-sume me.
is the Grove of Ten-der Touch-ing. To
p
27
sub. f
Oh, Cher-u-bi-no,
the west is the Riv - er of Sighs.

30
S
take me home.
I am un-worth-y of par - a - dise.
M-s
And south, past the arch - ing
mp non arp.
34
M-s
wil - low, is the Tem - ple of Love.
38
(Andante)
M-s
Come now, my dar - ling come with me,
Come to the room I have made for thee.

42
M-s
Let us strew the bed with flow - ers, There we will spend the hours.
46
M-s
There we will spend the hours. There we will spend the hours.
poco rall.
A tempo
p dolce
50
S
Yes, yes, my dar - ling, I'll come with thee, Come to the room that is made for me.
M-s
Come now, my dar - ling, come with me, Come to the room I have

54
S
Let us strew the bed with flow - ers, There we will spend the hours.
M-s
made for thee. Let us strew the bed with flow - ers, spend the hours.
58
S
There we will spend the hours. There we will spend the hours.
M-s
There we will spend the hours. There we will spend the hours.
mp
p
n
61
S
p
There we will
M-s
p
There we will

65
S
spend the hours. We will spend the
M-s
spend the hours. We will spend the
69
S
hours. There we will spend the hours
M-s
hours. There we will spend the hours
p

## Luigi Dallapiccola (1904–1975)

"Die Sonne kommt!," from *Goethe-lieder,* for voice and clarinets

Dallapiccola's *Goethe-lieder,* a work influenced by the twelve-tone music of Anton Webern, was composed in 1953 to texts by Johann Wolfgang von Goethe, whom many consider to be Germany's greatest poet. For an example of another Goethe setting, see Schubert's "Erlkönig" (p. 341).

Text by Johann Wolfgang von Goethe

*The part for piccolo clarinet is written at sounding pitch.

## TEXT AND TRANSLATION

"Die Sonne kommt!" from *Goethe-Lieder*

Die Sonne kommt! Ein Prachter scheinen!
Der Sichelmond umklammert sie.
Wer konnte solch ein Paar vereinen?
Dies Rätsel, wie erklärt sich's? wie?

"The Sun Comes Up!" from *Songs of Goethe*

The sun comes up! A glorious sight!
The crescent moon embraces her.
Who could unite such a pair?
This riddle, how to solve it? How?

## Claude Debussy (1862–1918)

"La cathédrale engloutie," from *Préludes,* Book I

"La cathédrale engloutie" ("The Engulfed Cathedral") is included in Debussy's first book of preludes, published in 1910, a collection of short programmatic piano pieces. Debussy's preludes, unlike earlier keyboard collections like Bach's *Well-Tempered Clavier* (p. 48) and Chopin's Preludes (p. 129), do not cycle through all the keys, but instead focus on poetic titles and musical imagery. The title of this prelude refers to a Breton legend of an underwater cathedral that sometimes rises to the ocean's surface.

From *Preludes for Piano, 1er Livre, par Claude Debussy.* Paris: Durand & Cie, Editeurs. 1910.

17
p marqué
pp
p marqué
pp
Augmentez progressivement (Sans presser)
19
p
marqué
21
f
8
24
8
più f
sff
Sonore sans duretè
28
8a bassa
8a bassa

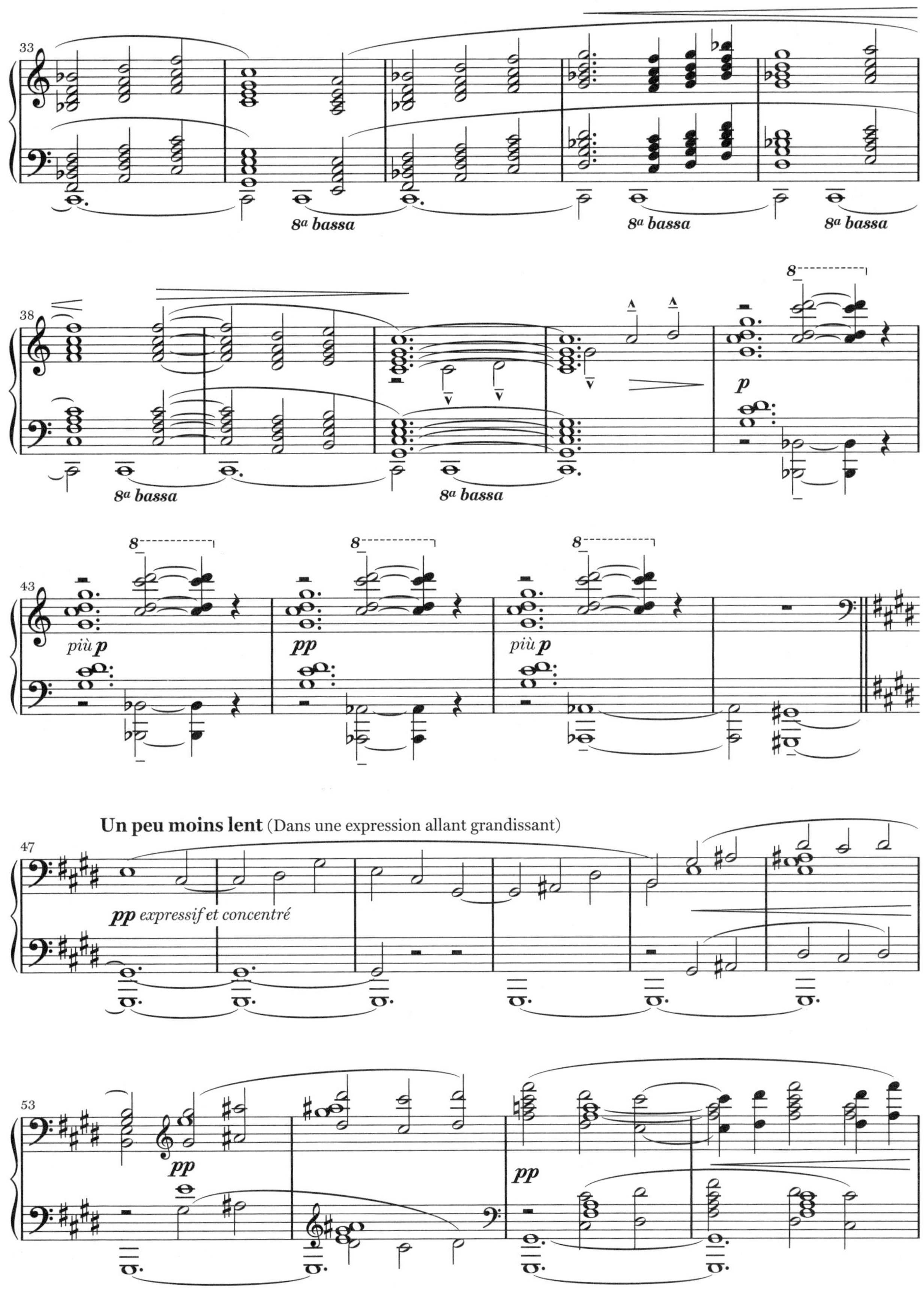
33
8a bassa
8a bassa
8a bassa
38
8a bassa
8a bassa
8
p
43
8
8
8
più p
pp
più p
Un peu moins lent (Dans une expression allant grandissant)
47
pp expressif et concentré
53
pp
pp

57
p
8
f
61
8
ff
molto dim.
p
65
p
70
pp
au Mouvt
pp Comme un écho de la phrase
entendue précédemment
8a bassa
Flottant et sourd
73
8a bassa

76
8a bassa
79
8a bassa
Dans la sonorité du début
82
più pp
pp
8a bassa
85
8
8
8

## "Down in the Valley"

"Down in the Valley" is a folk song that originated in the Ozark region of the south central United States. Though its date of composition cannot be known, it first appeared in print around 1910. The song tells of correspondence between a prisoner in a jail in Birmingham, Alabama, and a woman he loves. This arrangement, from an illustrated book of folk songs for families and children, *The Fireside Book of Folk Songs* (1947), omits the traditional second verse, which begins "Write me a letter, send it by mail, Send it in care of the Birmingham jail . . . ."

6
blow, Hang your head o - ver, hear the wind blow.
mine? An-swer my ques - tion, will you be mine?
you, An-gels in heav - en, know I love you.

## Gabriel Fauré (1845–1924)

### "Après un rêve"

"Après un rêve" ("After a Dream"), composed in 1877, is one of many art songs by Fauré, who is regarded as one of the most significant composers of French art song, or mélodie. The text, by an anonymous Tuscan poet and translated into French by Romain Bussine, recalls a dreamed encounter with a lover.

From *Gabriel Fauré: 20 Mélodies pour Piano et Chant.* Paris: Alphonse Leduc. n.d.

12
Tu ray - on - nais comme un ciel é-clairé par l'au-
Il bel - lo a - man - te m'ha fat - - to spa -
15
- ro - - re; Tu m'ap - pe -
- ri - - re, Se le ri -
18
- lais ___ et je quittais la ter - - re Pour m'enfuir a - vec
- tro - vo quell' a-mor gio con - - do Io mai più mi fa -
21
toi vers la lu - miè - - re,
- rò tra-dir del son - - - no,

24
Les cieux pour nous entr'ouvraient leurs nu - es, splen -
Se lo ri - tro - vo quell' a - mor gen - ti - le, mai
27
cresc. poco a poco.
- deurs in - con - nu - es, lu - eurs di - vi - nes en - tre -
più dal son - no, mi fa - rò tra -
30
f
- vu - es, Hé - las! Hé - las, triste réveil des
- di - re, Se lo ri - tro - vo quell' amor gio
33
son - - - ges Je t'ap - pel - le, ô
con - - - do. Se lo ri -

36
nuit, rends moi tes men - son - - - ges, Re -
- tro - vo quell' a mor gen - ti - - - le Mai
39
cresc.
- viens, re - viens ra - di - eu - - -
più mai più dal son - - -
f
42
p
- se. Re - viens, ô nuit mys - té - ri -
- no, dal son - - no mi fa - rò tra -
p
45
pp
- eu - - - - se!
- di - - - - re.
pp

## TEXT AND TRANSLATION

"Après un rêve"

Dans un sommeil que charmait ton image
Je rêvais le bonheur, ardent mirage,
Tes yeux étaient plus doux, ta voix pure et sonore,
Tu rayonnais comme un ciel éclairé par l'aurore;

Tu m'appelais et je quittais la terre
Pour m'enfuir avec toi vers la lumière,
Les cieux pour nous entr'ouvraient leurs nues,
Splendeurs inconnues, lueurs divines entrevues,

Hélas! Hélas! triste réveil des songes
Je t'appelle, ô nuit, rends moi tes mensonges,
Reviens, reviens radieuse,
Reviens ô nuit mystérieuse!

"After a Dream"

In a sleep that your image charmed,
I dreamed of happiness, ardent mirage,
Your eyes were softer, your voice pure and sonorous,
You shone like a sky lit by the dawn;

You called me and I left the earth
To run away with you toward the light,
The skies parted their clouds for us,
Splendors unknown, divine light glimpsed,

Alas, alas, sad awakening from the dreams,
I call you, O night, give me back your lies,
Return, return radiant,
Return, O mysterious night!

## Stephen Foster (1826–1864)

"Jeanie with the Light Brown Hair"

This song, published in 1854, exemplifies the music of Stephen Foster, an American composer of numerous parlor and minstrel songs, genres that were enormously popular in the nineteenth century. "Jeanie" is Jane McDowell, Foster's wife. Like many of Foster's songs "Jeanie with the Light Brown Hair" has become so well known that it is frequently assumed to be a folk song; the arrangement that appears here comes from *The Fireside Folksong Book,* a collection of American folk songs.

Arranged by Norman Lloyd

6
bright streams play,
joys gone by,
Hap - py as the dai - sies that dance on her way.
Sigh - ing round my heart o'er the fond hopes that die;
9
Man - y were the wild notes her mer - ry voice would pour,
Sigh - ing like the night wind and sob - bing like the rain,
Man - y were the blithe birds that
Wail - ing for the lost one that
12
war - bled them o'er;
comes not a - gain;
Ah!
Ah!
I dream of Jean - ie with the
I long for Jean - ie and my
mp

15
mp poco rit.
light brown_ hair, Float - ing, like a va - por, on the soft sum - mer air.
heart bows_ low, Nev - er more to find her where the bright wa - ters flow.
mp poco rit.

## George Gershwin (1898–1937)

"I Got Rhythm," from *Girl Crazy*

George and Ira Gershwin were composer-lyricist brothers, who wrote "I Got Rhythm" for a Broadway musical, *Girl Crazy,* in 1930. The song's chord progression, known as its "changes," has served as the basis for numerous jazz compositions, including works by Duke Ellington, Dizzie Gillespie, and Thelonious Monk.

Lyrics by Ira Gershwin

9
Gm Dm7 Gm Dm7 Gm Cm
buy. Birds in the tree sing Their
13
Gm6 E♭7 Gm Gm7 Cm7 F7
day - ful of song, Why should - n't we sing a -
17
B♭ Fm7 B♭ Fm7 B♭ D D7 Faug5 D7
long? I'm chip - per all the day,
sf
21
Cm7 E♭7 D D7 Faug5 D7
Hap - py with my lot. How do I get that way?
sf

25
Cm7
F7
Edim
G♭7
F7 B♭m6 Ddim F7
Look at what I've got:
f
Refrain
p-mf
29
B♭
B♭6
Cm7
F7
B♭6
Edim
Cm7
F7
I got rhy - thm,
I got mu - sic,
p-mf
33
B♭
B♭6
Cm7
F7
E♭m6
B♭
F7
B♭ C♯dim
F7
I got my man Who could ask for an - y-thing more?
37
B♭
B♭6
Cm7
F7
B♭6
Edim
Cm7
F7
I got dais - ies
In green pas - tures,

41
B♭ B♭6 Cm7 F7 E♭m6 B♭ F7 B♭
I got my man Who could ask for an-y-thing more?
45
D7 Am7 Dm7-5 D7 G Daug5 Dm G7
Old Man Troub-le, I don't mind him,
49
C7 Gm7 Cm7-5 C9 C7-5 F7 C7 F7
You won't find him 'Round my door.
53
B♭ B♭6 Cm7 F7 B♭6 Edim Cm7 F7
I got star-light, I got sweet dreams,

57
B♭
B♭6
Cm7
F7
E♭m
B♭
Fm
I got my man Who could ask for an - y - thing
60
G7
C7
F7
1.
B♭
A♭
G♭
D♭
2.
B♭
more, Who could ask for an - y-thing more?
more?
sfz
8

## George Gershwin

### "'S Wonderful!," from *Funny Face*

George and Ira Gershwin wrote "'S Wonderful!" in 1927 for the Broadway musical *Funny Face.* The musical starred Fred Astaire and was eventually made into a film. Though the film is radically different from the play, this song appears in both. The team wrote over two dozen Broadway and Hollywood shows, and in 1932 their "Of Thee I Sing" was awarded the Pulitzer Prize for drama.

Lyrics by Ira Gershwin

13
Cm Eb Am7-5 D7 Gm Bb7+5 Gm7-5 C7
How can words ex - press Your di - vine ap - peal?
When you said you care, 'Mag - ine my e - mosh;
17
Fm C Fm7-5 Bb Eb Bb Bbo C7
You can nev - er guess All the love I feel.
I swore then and there Per - ma - nent de - vosh.
21
Bb F9 F7 Bb Dbm6 Gb7
From now on la - dy I in - sist,
You made all oth - er boys seem blah;

25
B♭
F9
F7
Fm7
A♭m
B♭7
un poco rit.
For me no oth - er girls ex - ist.
Just you a - lone filled me with Aah!
un poco rit.
Refrain
29
p - mf
E♭
a tempo
E♭6
E♭
E♭6
C7
C♯°
C7
C♯°
'S won - der - ful!
'S mar vel - ous!
p - mf
a tempo
33
B♭7 (add6)
B♭7
E♭6
E♭
E♭6
E♭
You should care for me!

37
E♭ E♭6 E♭ E♭6 C7 C♯o C7 C♯o B♭(add6) B♭7
'S aw - ful nice 'S par - a - dise! 'S what I love to
43
E♭6 Am7-5 G D
see! You've made my life so
My dear, it's four - leaf
mf
47
G D7 Dm6 C7
cresc.
glam - or - ous You can't blame me for feel - ing
clo - ver time, From now on my heart's work - ing
cresc.

51
F7
B♭7
E♭
E♭6
E♭
E♭6
am - or - ous.
o - ver - time.
Oh!
'S won - der - ful!
55
Cm
F
Fm7
E°
Fm7
B♭7
'S mar - vel - ous!
That you should care for
59
1.
E♭ Gm Fm A♭ Gm Cm Fm7 B♭
2.
E♭ A♭ E♭
me!
me!

## "Greensleeves"

"Greensleeves" is a traditional English folk song; though its date of composition is unknown, it is first mentioned in print in 1580. The music originally accompanied a ballad about a woman, referred to as Lady Greensleeves, who discourteously rejects a suitor. The music has also been used to set numerous other texts, including the well-known Christmas carol "What Child Is This?" Excerpts from two arrangements for solo guitar are shown here.

Arranged by John Duarte

Arranged by Norbert Kraft

9
13

## George Frideric Handel (1685–1759)

Chaconne in G Major

This Chaconne, a revised version of a composition Handel wrote in 1705, appeared in a collection of his harpsichord music published in 1733. Handel lived in an era without copyright laws, and he produced the 1733 collection to compete with pirated editions of his works (including the Chaconne) that were already in circulation. Like all chaconnes, Handel's consists of variations on a repeated harmonic pattern.

From *George Frideric Handel: Keyboard Works for Solo Instrument*. New York: Dover Publications, Inc.

29
tr
tr
33
Var. 4.
37
tr
tr
41
Var. 5.
45
49
Var. 6.

53
Var. 7.
57
61
tr
65
Var. 8.
69
Var. 9.
Adagio.
73

Var. 10.
81
89
Var. 11.
93
97
Var. 12.
101
tr
105
Var. 13.
109

Var. 14.
113
117
Var. 15.
121
125
Var. 16.
129
133
Var. 17.
137

141
145
Var. 18.
150
Var. 19.
155
159
Var. 20.
163
167
Var. 21.

171
tr

## George Frideric Handel

From *Messiah*

Handel's *Messiah,* composed in 1741, is an example of an oratorio—an unstaged, usually sacred vocal work that tells a story. After studying in Italy, the German-born Handel began his career in London as an opera composer, writing popular Italian operas; by the 1740s, tastes had shifted and he turned his attention to oratorios. *Messiah* tells the story of the life of Jesus, using texts from the Christian Bible. It is one of the most widely performed oratorios today, with numerous choral organizations presenting annual performances (often in abridged versions). Two solo movements are shown below: an aria for soprano and a recitative for tenor.

### "Rejoice greatly"

10
joice, re-joice great-ly, re - joice,
mf
13
O daugh-ter of Zi - on!
mf
16
O daugh-ter of Zi-on! re - joice, re - joice,
p
19
re-joice!

22
25
O daugh - ter of Zi - on! Re - joice great - ly,
28
shout,
O daugh - ter of Je - ru - sa - lem:
30
be - hold, thy king com - eth un - to thee,

33
be - hold, thy king com-eth un - to thee, com-eth
p
36
un - to thee.
f
39
42
p
f

Meno mosso
44
He is the right - eous Sav - ior.
p
47
and he shall speak peace un-to the hea -
p
50
then, he shall speak peace, he shall speak peace,
53
peace, he shall speak peace un-to the hea - then,

56
he is the right - eous Sav - ior, and he shall
59
speak, he shall speak peace, peace,
62
he shall speak peace un - to the hea -
65
then. Re - joice, re -
a tempo
f
p

68
joice, re - joice great - ly,
f
71
re - joice
p
74
great - ly, O daugh - ter of
mf
p
77
Zi - on! shout, O daugh-ter of Je - ru - sa - lem!
mf
p
mf

80
Be - hold, thy king com - eth un - to thee, re - joice,
p
83
re - joice
mf
p
mf
86
and shout, shout, shout, shout, re - joice
p
89
great - ly,
f

92
re - joice great - ly, O daugh - ter of Zi - on! shout,
p
95
O daugh-ter of Je - ru - sa-lem! Be-hold, thy king com-eth un - to
98
ad lib.
thee, be-hold, thy king com - eth un - to thee.
a tempo
colla voce
f
101
103
tr

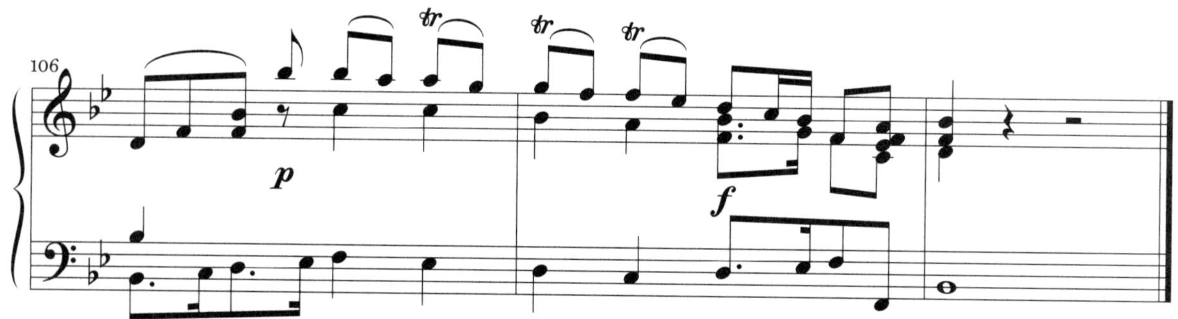
106
p
f

# "Thy rebuke hath broken His heart"

## Joseph Haydn (1732–1809)

Piano Sonata No. 9 in F Major, third movement

This Scherzo is the final movement of a short piano sonata that Haydn composed sometime before 1766. He originally titled this simple sonata a "divertimento" (or "diversion").

From *Joseph Haydn: Complete Piano Sonatas, Volume I*. New York: Dover Publications, Inc.

## Joseph Haydn

String Quartet in D Minor, Op. 76, No. 2 (*Quinten*), Menuetto and Trio

Haydn was one of the first composers to write for string quartet, a genre to which he frequently returned, publishing numerous collections of quartets. The *Quinten* ("Fifths") Quartet is part of a collection published in 1797. Its name comes from the quartet's first movement, which makes prominent use of perfect fifths. The menuetto is unusual in that it combines a contrapuntal technique, a strict canon, with a Classical binary form.

From *Joseph Haydn: Eleven Late String Quartets, Opp. 74, 76, and 77, Complete.* New York: Dover Publications, Inc.

19
25
32
1.
2.
38
Trio.
p sempre stacc.
cresc.
f
ff

47
1.
2.
p
p
p
p
p
53
p
p
p
p
59
66
f
cresc.
ff
f
cresc.
ff
f
cresc.
ff
f
cresc.
ff

74
8
p
p
p
M. D. C.

## Fanny Mendelssohn Hensel (1805–1847)

"Bitte," Op. 7, No. 5

Fanny Mendelssohn Hensel and her brother, Felix Mendelssohn, were raised in a musical household. Fanny was encouraged to compose by her brother, whose works she influenced. Because there were few publication opportunities for women composers, Hensel published some of her songs under her brother's name, but in 1846, near the end of her life, she published one volume of Lieder in her own name. "Bitte" and "Nachtwanderer" appear in a collection of songs by Hensel published in 1848, a year after her death. The song's text is by the Austrian poet Nikolaus Lenau.

Text by Nikolaus Lenau

8
gründ - lich sü - sse Nacht, ern - ste mil - de träu - me -
schwe - best für und für, dass du ü - ber mei - nem
11
rei - che, un - er - gründ - lich sü - sse Nacht un - er -
Le - ben, ein - sam schwe - best für und für ein - sam
15
1.
2.
gründ - lich sü - sse Nacht.
schwe - best für und für.

## TEXT AND TRANSLATION

"Bitte"

Weil' auf mir, du dunkles Auge,
Übe deine ganze Macht,
Ernste milde träumereiche,
Unergründlich süsse Nacht.

Nimm mit deinem Zauberdunkel
Diese Welt von hinnen mir,
Dass du über meinem Leben
Einsam schwebest für und für.

"Please"

Dwell on me, you dark eyes,
Exert your entire power,
Solemn, tender, dreamy,
Unfathomably sweet night.

Take with your dark magic
This world away from me,
That over my life
You alone hold sway forever and ever.

## Fanny Mendelssohn Hensel

"Nachtwanderer," Op. 7, No. 1

"Nachtwanderer" is a setting of a poem by Joseph Karl Benedikt von Eichendorff, a German lyric poet whose writings were often set by composers.

Text by Joseph Karl Benedikt von Eichendorff

Andante con moto
p
Ich wand - re durch die stil - le
p
4
Nacht, da schleicht der Mond so heim - lich sacht
7
oft aus der dun - keln Wol - - - - ken - hül - - le.
Ped.

10
cresc.
Und hin und her im Tal
cresc.
er-wacht die Nach - ti -
cresc.
13
p
gall,
dann wie - der al - les grau, al - les
p
16
grau und stil - - le.
O
19
cresc.
f
wun - der-ba - rer Nacht - ge - sang,
von fern im Land der Strö - me Gang,
cresc.
p trem.

23
p
pp
l'istesso tempo
cresc.
leis' Schau-ern in den dun - keln Bäu-men, irrst die Ge-
27
f
dan-ken mir, mein wir-res Sin-gen hier ist wie ein
31
dim.
p
cresc.
Ru - fen nur aus Träu - - - - - - men, mein Sin - gen ist ein
35
pp
cresc.
Ru - - - fen, ein Ru - - fen nur aus Träu - - - men.

## TEXT AND TRANSLATION

"Nachtwanderer"

Ich wandre durch die stille Nacht,
Da schleicht der Mond so heimlich sacht
Oft aus der dunkeln Wolkenhülle.
Und hin und her im Tal
Erwacht die Nachtigall,
Dann wieder alles grau und stille.

O wunderbarer Nachtgesang,
Von fern im Land der Ströme Gang,
Leis' Schauern in den dunkeln Bäumen,
Irrst die Gedanken mir,
Mein wirres Singen hier
Ist wie ein Rufen nur aus Träumen,
Mein Singen is ein Rufen,
Ein Rufen nur aus Träumen.

"Night Wanderer"

I wander through the still night;
There creeps the moon so secretly, gently,
Often out from the dark cloud cover.
And here and there in the valley
Wakes the nightingale,
Then again all is gray and still.

O wonderful night song,
From afar in the land where the currents flow,
Soft shuddering in the dark trees
Confuses my thoughts.
My wild singing here
Is like a cry only from dreams;
My singing is a cry,
A cry only from dreams.

## Fanny Mendelssohn Hensel

"Neue Liebe, neues Leben"

"Neue Liebe, neues Leben," a setting of a poem by Johann Wolfgang von Goethe, is one of many songs by Hensel that were unpublished during her lifetime. As this book is going to press, the anthology recording is the only commercially available performance of this lovely song.

Text by Johann Wolfgang von Goethe

13
rit.
*f* a tempo
Fleiß und_ dei - ne Ruh', ach, wie kamst du_ nur da - zu? Fes - selt_
rit.
a tempo
17
dich die Ju - gend - blü - te, die - se_ lieb - li - che Ge - stalt,_ die - ser_
21
Blick voll Treu' und_ Gü - te, mit un - end - li - cher_ Ge - walt.
26
*p*
Will ich rasch mich ihr ent - zie - hen, mich er - man - nen, ihr ent - flie - hen, füh - ret_
*p*

31
mich im Au - gen - blick, ach, mein Weg zu ihr zu - rück, füh - ret mich im Au - gen -
36
- blick, ach, mein Weg zu ihr zu - rück, zu ihr zu -
dolce
41
- rück. Und an die - sem Zau - ber Fäd - chen, das sich nicht zer - rei - ßen läßt, hält das
46
lie - be, lo - se Mäd - chen mich so wi - der Wil - len fest, hält das lie - be,

51
pp
f a tempo
lo - se Mäd-chen mich so wi - - - der Wil-len fest; muß in
a tempo
pp
f
57
ih - rem Zau-ber - krei-se le - ben nun auf ih - re Wei-se, ach wie groß, ach wie
62
groß, Lie - be, Lie - be laß mich los, laß mich los, laß mich los, Lie-be,
67
cresc.
ff
Lie - be laß mich los, laß mich los, laß mich los, Lie-be, Lie - - be
cresc.
ff

72
laß, oh _ laß _ mich los!

## TEXT AND TRANSLATION

"Neue Liebe, neues Leben"

Herz, mein Herz, was soll das geben?
Was bedränget dich so sehr?
Welch' ein fremdes neues Leben,
Ich erkenne dich nicht mehr.

Weg ist alles, was du liebtest,
Weg, worum du dich betrübtest,
Weg dein Fleiß und deine Ruh',
Ach, wie kamst du nur dazu?

Fesselt dich die Jugendblüte,
Diese liebliche Gestalt,
Dieser Blick voll Treu' und Güte,
Mit unendlicher Gewalt?

Will ich rasch mich ihr entziehen,
Mich ermannen, ihr entfliehen,
Führet mich im Augenblick
Ach, mein Weg zu ihr zurück.

Und an diesem Zauberfädchen,
Das sich nicht zerreißen läßt,
Hält das liebe, lose Mädchen
Mich so wider Willen fest;

Muß in ihrem Zauberkreise
Leben nun auf ihre Weise.
[Die Verändrung], ach wie groß,
Liebe, Liebe, laß mich los!

"New Love, New Life"

Heart, my heart, what does this mean?
What troubles you so much?
What a strange new life!
I don't recognize you any more.

Gone is all that you loved,
Gone is what troubled you,
Gone your hard work and your peace,
Ah, how did you come to this?

Are you captivate of youth's bloom,
This lovely form,
This gaze full of faithfulness and goodness,
With infinite power?

If I swiftly run away from her
To take courage, to flee from her,
At that moment,
Ah, my way leads me back to her.

And with this magic thread,
Which cannot be cut,
The sweet, mischievous maiden
Holds me so tightly against my will;

I must in her magic circle
Live now in her manner.
[The transformation], oh how great,
Love, love, let me go!

## Hymn tunes

### "America" ("My Country, 'Tis of Thee")

The tune for "America" was first sung as the British national anthem, "God Save the Queen" (or King), in the eighteenth century. It has since been adapted as a patriotic song in the United States and in many other Anglophone nations. The words were written in 1831 by Samuel Francis Smith, but have been changed (to "God Save George Washington," for example) from the time of the American Revolution.

1. My coun - try, 'tis of thee, Sweet land of lib - er - ty,
2. My na - tive coun - try, thee, Land of the no - ble free,
5
Of thee I sing; Land where my fa - thers died, Land of the
Thy name I love; I love thy rocks and rills, Thy woods and
10
pil - grims' pride, From ev - ery moun - tain - side Let free - dom ring.
tem - pled hills; My heart with rap - ture thrills Like that a - bove.

## "Chartres"

This tune, named for a town in France, is a French folk melody from the fifteenth century that was later harmonized by Charles Wood, a nineteenth-century English composer. The tune is most often sung to the words of the hymn "Saw You Never, in the Twilight," of which one verse is shown below. This hymn and those that follow are shown using traditional hymn notation: double bars at the end of each phrase indicate to the congregation where to breathe. Here, the measure at the end of the phrase is not complete until after the anacrusis for the following phrase, as reflected in the measure numbering.

## "Old Hundredth"

This tune appeared in the Geneva Psalter, a collection of melodies that were used in Calvinist churches for singing texts from the book of Psalms. The name "Old Hundredth" indicates that this music was used to set Psalm 100. Both the melody and its harmonization are probably by Louis Bourgeois, a French composer who played an important role in gathering Calvinist hymns.

1. All peo - ple that on earth do dwell, sing to the Lord with
2. Know that the Lord is God in - deed; with - out our aid he
3. O en - ter then his gates with praise, ap - proach with joy his
cheer - ful voice: Him serve with mirth, his praise forth
did us make: we are his folk, he doth us
courts un - to; praise, laud, and bless his Name al -
tell, come ye be - fore him and re - joice.
feed, and for his sheep he doth us take. A - men.
ways, for it is seem - ly so to do.

## "Rosa Mystica"

"Rosa Mystica" is a German Christmas carol, better known in English as "Lo, How a Rose E'er Blooming." This version was harmonized in 1609 by Michael Praetorius, a composer and collector of Lutheran church music. No meter signature is provided because this hymn tune predates the current system of meter signatures: some measures imply $\frac{4}{4}$ and $\frac{3}{4}$ with a quarter-note beat unit; others $\frac{3}{2}$ or $\frac{2}{2}$ with a half-note beat unit.

## "St. Anne Chorale"

The English composer William Croft wrote and harmonized this tune in 1708. Most often, it is sung as the hymn "O God Our Help in Ages Past" to words written by Isaac Watts in 1719, based on Psalm 90. The tune bears such a strong resemblance to the opening subject of Bach's Fugue in E♭ Major for organ (p. 32), composed in 1739, that Bach's work is now known as the "St. Anne" Fugue.

1
1. O God, our help in a - ges past, Our hope for years to come,
2. Be - fore the hills in or - der stood, Or earth re - ceived her frame,
5
Our shel - ter from the storm - y blast, And our e - ter - nal home:
From ev - er - last - ing thou art God, To end - less years the same.

## "St. George's Windsor"

George J. Elvey, who was organist at St. George's Church in Windsor, England, composed this tune in 1858. Though it was originally written for the text "Hark, the Song of Jubilee," the music is now most frequently sung to the text "Come, Ye Thankful People Come," adapted from a poem by Henry Alford, penned in 1844. In the United States, this hymn is typically sung at Thanksgiving.

1. Come, ye thank - ful peo - ple, come, Raise the song of har - vest-home:
2. All the world is God's own field, Fruit un - to his praise to yield;
All is safe - ly gath - ered in, Ere the win - ter storms be - gin;
Wheat and tares to - geth - er sown, Un - to joy or sor - row grown:
God, our Ma - ker, doth pro - vide For our wants to be sup - plied;
First the blade, and then the ear, Then the full corn shall ap - pear:
Come to God's own tem - ple, come, Raise the song of har - vest - home.
Grant, O har - vest Lord, that we Whole-some grain and pure may be.

## **Scott Joplin (1868–1917)**

"Pine Apple Rag"

Joplin's "Pine Apple Rag," named for the town Pine Apple, Alabama, was published in 1908. Like all ragtime, this composition makes use of the "ragged rhythms," or syncopations, that characterize the genre and are common to much African-American music written and performed around the turn of the century.

From *Scott Joplin: Complete Piano Rags*. New York: Dover Publications, Inc.

17
f
1
19
2
mf
23
28
33
f
1
2

37
mf
f
42
mf
47
f
52
mp
57
mf
mp

62
67
1
2
mf
71
76
81
1
2
Fine.

## Scott Joplin

"Solace"

"Solace," published in 1909, is not a typical rag, though it does make use of the syncopation that characterizes ragtime. It is sometimes listed with the subtitle "A Mexican Serenade," and it bears some resemblance to the tango. Like other Joplin compositions, "Solace" was made famous by its inclusion in the 1973 film *The Sting*, starring Paul Newman and Robert Redford.

From *Scott Joplin: Complete Piano Rags*. New York: Dover Publications, Inc.

17
1
2
21
3
f Ped.
mp
25
3
f Ped.
29
Ped.
Ped.
Ped.
34
1
2
mp
Ped.

37
mf
41
45
49
53
mp
57
a tempo
mf
mp

61
a tempo
65
1
2
69
f
73
77
81
1
2
Fine.

## Wolfgang Amadeus Mozart (1756–1791)

From *The Marriage of Figaro:* "Quanto duolmi, Susanna" (recitative) and "Voi, che sapete" (aria)

Mozart's opera *The Marriage of Figaro* received its premiere in 1786 in Vienna. Here, the character Cherubino sings about his chronic love sickness. Though Cherubino is a male character, Mozart wrote the music for a woman to sing; when a woman portrays a young man on the operatic stage, her part is called a "pants role." In performances of this opera, cuts are typically made to shorten its duration. Indications in the score show the cuts made in the recording that accompanies this text.

Libretto by Lorenzo da Ponte

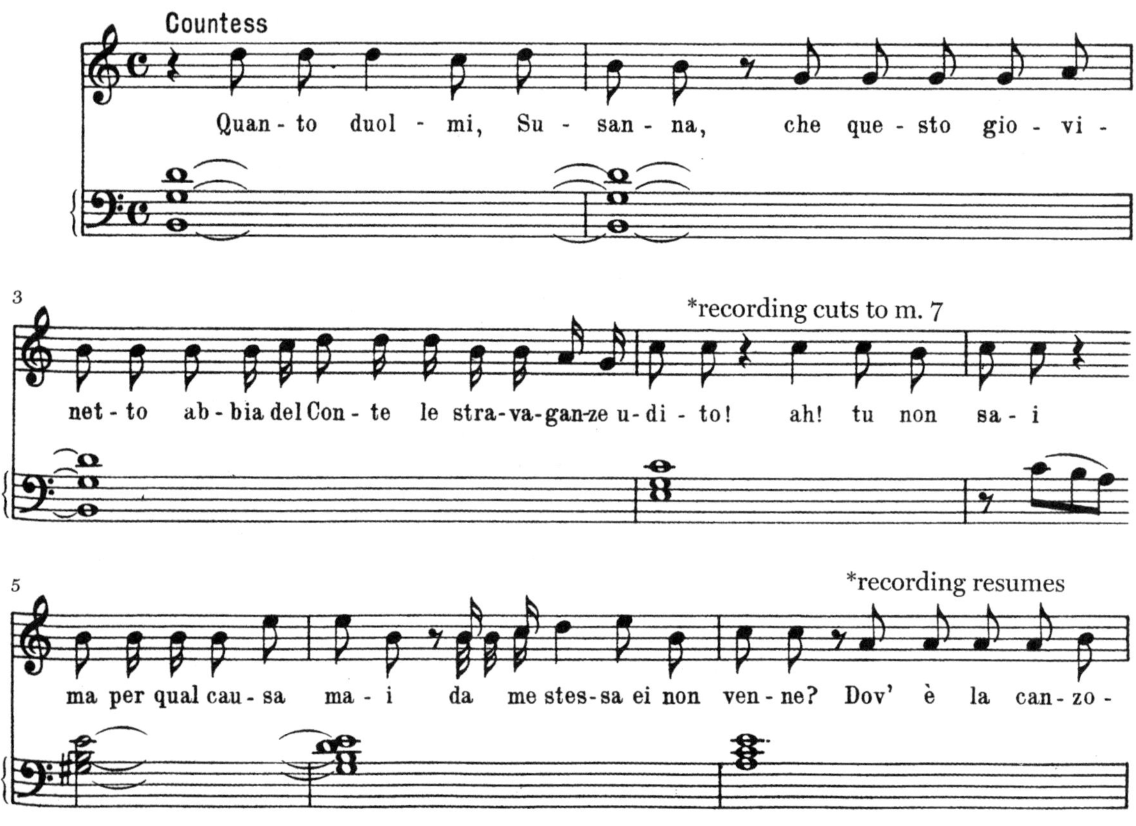

8
Susanna
net - ta? Ec - co - la, ap - pun - to fac - ciam che ce la can - ti. Zit - to, vien
*recording cuts to m. 19
10
(Enter Cherubino.)
Cherubino
gen - te, è des - so: a - van - ti, a - van - ti, si - gnor uf - fi - zi - a - le! Ah, non chia -
12
mar - mi con no - me sì fa - ta - le! ei mi ram - men - ta, che ab -
14
Susanna
ban - do - nar degg' - i - o co - ma - re tan - to buo - na! E tan - to
16
Cherubino (sighing)
Susanna (mocking him)
bel - la. Ah sì, cer - to! Ah sì, cer - to! i - po - cri -

19
*recording resumes
to - ne! via pre - sto la can - zo - ne, che sta-ma-ne a me de - ste,
21
Countess
Susanna (pointing to Cherubino)
a ma-da - ma can-ta - te. Chi n'è l'au-tor? Guar - da - te, e-gli ha due
23
Countess
bra - ci di ros - sor sul - la fac - cia. Pren-di la mia chi -
25
Cherubino
tar - ra, e l'ac-com-pa - gna. Io so - no sì tre - man - te,
27
Susanna
ma se ma-da - ma vuo-le— Lo vuo - le, sì, lo vuol, man-co pa - ro - le.

Andante con moto (Susanna plays the Ritornello on the guitar.)
p
5
9
Cherubino
Voi, che sa - pe - te che co - sa è a - mor,
13
Don - ne, ve - de - te, s'io l'ho nel cor,
3

17
Don - ne, ve - de - te, s'io l'ho nel cor.
21
Quel - lo ch'io pro - vo, vi ri - di - ro,
25
È per me nuo - vo ca - pir nol so.
29
Sen - to un af - fet - to pien di de - sir,

33
Ch'o - ra è di - let - to, ch'o - ra è mar - tir.
37
Ge - lo, e poi sen - to l'al - ma av-vam - par,
41
E in un mo - men - to___ tor - no a ge - lar.
45
Ri - cer - co un be - ne fuo - ri di me,

49
Non so chi il tie - ne, non so cos' è. So - spi - ro e
53
ge - mo sen - za vo - ler, Pal - pi - to e tre - mo sen - za sa -
fp
56
per. Non tro - vo pa - ce not - te, nè dì, Ma pur mi pia - ce
mfp
60
lan - guir co - sì. Voi, che sa - pe - te

64
che co - sa è a - mor, Don - ne, ve - de - te,
3
68
s'io l'ho nel cor, Don - ne, ve - de - te,
3
72
s'io l'ho nel cor, Don - ne, ve - de - te,
76
s'io l'ho nel cor.
tr
tr

## TEXT AND TRANSLATION

Countess:
Quanto duolmi, Susanna,
Che questo giovinetto abbia
Del Conte le stravaganze udito!
Ah! tu non sai ma per qual causa mai
Da me stessa ei non venne?
Dov' è la canzonetta?

How I grieve, Susanna,
That this young man has
Heard the extravagant stories of the count!
Ah, you don't know yet why he did not
See me himself in person?
Where is the love song?

Susanna:
Eccola,
Apppunto facciam che ce la canti.
Zitto, vien gente, è desso;
Avanti, avanti, signor uffiziale!

Here it is,
As soon as he comes, we will have him sing it.
Quiet, someone's coming, it's him—
Come in, come in, mister officer!

Cherubino:
Ah, non chiamarmi con nome sì fatale!
Ei mi rammenta, che abbandonar
Degg'io comare tanto buona!
E tanto bella. Ah sì, certo!

Oh, do not call me with that fatal title!
And that reminds me that I must soon
Abandon my good lady!
And so beautiful. Ah yes, of course!

Susanna:
Ah sì, certo!
Ipocritone!
Via presto la canzone,
Che stamane a me deste,
A madama cantate.

Ah yes, of course!
Hypocrite!
Now quickly sing that love song
You gave me this morning,
Sing to Madame.

Countess:
Chi n'è l'autor?

Who is the author?

Susanna:
Guardate, egli ha due braci
Di rossor sulla faccia.

Look, he has two blushing embers
On his face.

Countess:
Prendi la mia chitarra, e l'accompagna.

Take my guitar and accompany him.

Cherubino:
Io sono sì tremante, ma se madama vuole—

I am trembling, but if Madame wishes—

Susanna:
Lo vuole, sì, lo vuol, manco parole.

She wishes, yes, she wishes—no more talk.

Voi, che sapete che cosa è amor,
Donne, vedete s'io l'ho nel cor.
Quello ch'io provo vi ridirò,
è per me nuovo, capir nol so.
Sento un affetto pien di desir,
Ch'ora è diletto, ch'ora è martir.
Gelo e poi sento l'alma avvampar,
E in un momento torno a gelar.
Ricerco un bene fuori di me,
Non so chi'l tiene, non so cos'è.
Sospiro e gemo senza voler,
Palpito e tremor senza saper.
Non trovo pace notte nè dì,
Ma pur mi piace languir così.
Voi, che sapete che cosa è amor,
Donne, vedete s'io l'ho nel cor.

You who know what love is,
Ladies, see if I have it in my heart.
What I feel I will recount to you,
And for me it is new, I cannot understand it.
I feel an emotion, full of desire,
Which now is pleasure, which now is suffering.
I freeze and then I feel my soul burning up,
And in a minute I am freezing again.
I search for a good thing outside of me,
I don't know how to take it; I don't know what it is.
I sigh and moan without wanting to,
Throb and tremble without knowing why.
I find no peace night or day,
Yet I enjoy languishing this way.
You who know what love is,
Ladies, see if I have it in my heart.

## Wolfgang Amadeus Mozart

Minuet in F Major, K. 2

This minuet, which Mozart wrote in 1762 when he was six years old, is typical of the small-scale keyboard works that make up many of the early compositions of this child prodigy. Mozart's composition appears in a notebook of piano pieces for his older sister, Maria Anna Mozart.

## Wolfgang Amadeus Mozart

Piano Sonata in G Major, K. 283, first movement

Mozart composed this sonata in 1774 while in Munich for performances of his early opera *La finta giardiniera* (*The Pretend Garden-Maid*). It appears in his first published collection of piano sonatas. The recording that accompanies this anthology was made on a fortepiano, the type of instrument on which Mozart would have performed and for which he composed.

From *Wolfgang Amadeus Mozart: Complete Sonatas and Fantasies for Solo Piano.* New York: Dover Publications, Inc.

34
38
p
f
43
tr
p
48
f
52
p
59
f
p
65
f
p
f
p

72
80
86
92
97
103
108
f
p
tr

112
p
f
117

## Wolfgang Amadeus Mozart

Piano Sonata in D Major, K. 284, third movement

This sonata was written in 1774 for the Baron von Dürnitz. The recording on the disc that accompanies this anthology was made on a fortepiano, which allows for striking changes in timbre and dynamic levels between variations.

From *Wolfgang Amadeus Mozart: Complete Sonatas and Fantasies for Solo Piano.* New York: Dover Publications, Inc.

VAR. II.
VAR. III.

57
60
p
f
62
p
f
66
p
cresc.
f
VAR. IV.
69
f
71
74

77
p
legato
f
79
82
VAR. V.
86
(f)
91
p
f
96
p
f
p
f
VAR. VI. 103
f

107
111
113
117
VAR. VII.
Minore.
120
p
tr
f
123
p
cresc.
f
p
128
p
f
p

132
tr
tr
p
VAR. VIII.
Maggiore.
137
p
f
141
145
p
f
p
149
f
VAR. IX.
154
p
f
159
p
p
f
p

165
VAR. X.
171
174
179
183
VAR. XI.
Adagio cantabile.
Nach den ältesten Ausgaben.
[According to the earliest editions]
188
(Nach dem Autograph.) [According to the MS]
legato

191
194
197
tr
199
201
p

204
208
212
214
217
tr
(tr)

219
VAR. XII.
(Allegro.)
222
(f)
p
229
f
legato
234
p
239
f
decresc.
p
f
p
246
f
p
pp
251
f
legato

256

## Wolfgang Amadeus Mozart

Piano Sonata in C Major, K. 545

Mozart wrote this sonata in 1788 and characterized it as "for beginners." It was not published until 1805, after Mozart's death. Even today, this work is one of the first sonatas assigned to young pianists and is one of his works best known by amateur performers. All three movements are included on the recordings, in two performances: on fortepiano and on a modern piano, for comparison.

From *Wolfgang Amadeus Mozart: Complete Sonatas and Fantasies for Solo Piano.* New York: Dover Publications, Inc.

tr
25
f
29
f
33
36
39
decresc.
42
p
tr
47

50
53
cresc.
56
f
p
legato
60
tr
tr
63
66
cresc.
70
tr
f

Andante.
p dolce
legato
4
7
f
legato
11
14
dim.
dolce
18
21
f
fp

25
f
29
fp
33
p
36
37
f
39
42
45
f

48
legato
52
56
60
64
68
71
p
f
mf
dim.
sf
sfp

RONDO.
Allegretto.
mf
p
f
5
mf
legato
10
p
15
21
mf
p
f
27
p
mf
33
sf
f

38
p
43
sfp
p
48
cresc.
poco f
53
p
f
59
legato
64
f
69

## Wolfgang Amadeus Mozart

From *Requiem:* Kyrie eleison and Dies irae

This Kyrie movement is from Mozart's *Requiem,* a mass for a Catholic funeral service. Written in 1791, the mass was left unfinished at his death, and was completed by Franz Xavier Süssmayer, a Viennese composer who may have studied with Mozart. In the film adaptation of Peter Shaffer's play *Amadeus,* the *Requiem* is famously (and fictionally) composed by Mozart's rival Antonio Salieri, from themes sung to him by Mozart on his deathbed.

From *Wolfgang Amadeus Mozart: Requiem.* C. F. Peters. n.d.

7
F
-i - son, e - le - - i - son, e - le -
f
Ky - ri - e e - le - i - son, e -
-i - son, e - le - - i - son!
e e - le - - i - son, e - le - i - son! Christe e - le -
F
10
- i - son, e - le - - i - son! Christe e -
le - - i - son, e - le - i - son,
Ky - ri - e e - le - i -
- i - son, e -
13
G
le - - i -
e - le - - i - son, e - le - i - son, e -
son, e - le -
le - - i - son, e - le - i - son, e - le - i - son,
G

16
son! Ky- -ri -e e- -le- -i- son, e- le-
le- -i- son! Ky- ri- e e- lei- son, e- lei- son,
-i- son, e- le- -i- son!
e- le- -i- son! Christe e- le-
19
H
-i- son! Christe e- le-
e- le- -i- son! Christe e- le-
Ky- -ri- e e- -le- -i- son, e-
-i- son!
H Trombe.
22
-i- son!
-i- son! Chri- ste e-
le- -i-
Ky- -ri- e e- -le- -i

25
I
Ky - ri -
le - - - - - - - - - - - - - - - - - - i -
son, e - le - - - - - - - - - - - - - - i -
son, e - le - - - - - - - - - - - - - - - - - - i -
I
1
3
5
28
e e - le - i - son, e - le - - - - - - - i -
son, e - le i - son, e - le - - - - - - - - - - i - son!
son! Christe e - le - - - - - - - i - son! Christe e -
son, e - le - i - son! Ky - ri - e e - le - i -
31
K
son, e - le - - - - i - son, e - le - - i - son,
Ky - ri - e e - le - i -
le - - - - - - - - - - - - i - son, e - le - i - son!
son, e - le - - - - - - - - - i - son! Christe e -
K

34
L
e - le - - - - i - son! Chri - ste e -
son! Chri - ste e - le - - - - - - i -
Chri - ste e - le - - - - - - i - son, e - le - - - - - i -
le - - - - - - i - son, e - le - - - - i - son!
L
37
le - - - - - - i - son, e - le - - - - - i - son!
son, e - le - - - - - i - son! Ky - ri - e e - lei - son, e - le - - -
son, e - le - i - son! Ky - ri - e, Ky - ri - e e - le - i -
Chri - ste e - le - - - - - - - - i - son! Ky - ri - e e -
Trombe, Timp.
40
M
Christe e - le - - - - - - - - - - - - - - i - son, e -
- - i - son, e - lei - - son! Ky - ri - e e -
son! Ky - ri - e e - le - i - son, e - le - - - - - i - son, e -
le - i - son, e - le - - - - - - - - - - i - son, e -
M

43
N
le - i - son, e - le - i - son!
Chri - ste e -
le - i - son! Ky - ri - e e - le - i - son, e - le - i -
le - i - son, e - le - i - son, e - le - i - son, e -
le - i - son!
Chri - ste e - le - i -
N
46
le - i - son! Chri - ste e - le -
son! Chri - ste e - le - i - son! Ky - ri - e, Ky - ri -
le - i - son, e - le - i - son, e - le - i - son! Ky - ri - e, Ky - ri -
son, e - le - i - son, e - le - i - son, e - le - i - son, e - le -
49
Adagio.
- i - son, e - le - i - son! Ky - ri - e e - le - i - son!
e e - le - i son! Ky - ri - e e - le - i son!
e e - le - i son! Ky - ri - e e - le - i - son!
- i - son, e - le - i - son! Ky - ri - e e - le - i - son!
Trombe, Timp.
Adagio.

Allegro assai.
Tutti.
Soprano.
Alto.
Tenore.
Basso.
Di - - es i - rae di - - - - es
Allegro assai.
Orchestral reduction
Volles Orch.
4
il - la solvet sae_clum in fa - vil - la, te - ste Da - vid cum Sy -
il - la solvet sae_clum in fa - vil - la, te_ste Da - vid cum Sy -
8
bil - - la.
Quan - - - - - tus
Quan - - - - - tus,

11
tre - mor est fu - tu - - - rus, quan - - - - - do
tre - mor est fu - tu - - - rus, quan - - - - - do
quan - - - - tus tre - mor est fu - tu - - - - rus,
tre - mor est fu - tu - - - rus, quan - - - - - do
14
ju - dex est ven - tu - - - rus, cun - - - cta
ju - dex est ven - tu - - - rus, cun - - - cta
quan - - - - do ju - dex est ven - tu - - rus, cun - - - cta
ju - dex est ven - tu - - rus, cun - - - cta
17
stri - - - cte dis - cus - su - - - rus.
stri - - - - cte dis - cus - su - - - rus.
stri - cte stri - cte dis - cus - su - - - rus.
stri - - - cte dis - cus - su - - - rus.
Streichinstr.

20
P
Di - - - es
Di - - - es
Di - - - es
Di - - - es
P Tutti.
23
i - rae di - - - - es il - la solvet saeclum in fa-
i - rae di - - - - es il - la solvet saeclum in fa-
i - rae di - - - - es il - la solvet saeclum in fa-
i - rae di - - - - es il - la solvet saeclum in fa-
27
vil - la te - ste Da - vid cum Sy - bil - la.
vil - la te - ste Da - vid cum Sy - bil - la.
vil - la te - ste Da - vid cum Sy - bil - la.
vil - la te - ste Da - vid cum Sy - bil - la.
tr

30
Q
Quan - - - - tus tre - mor est fu -
Quan - - - - tus tre - mor est fu -
Quan - - - - tus tre - mor est fu -
Quan - - - - tus tre - mor est fu -
Q
33
tu - - rus quan - - - - - do ju - dex est ven -
tu - - rus quan - - - - - do ju - dex est ven -
tu - - rus quan - - - - - do ju - dex est ven -
tu - - rus quan - - - - - do ju - dex est ven -
36
tu - rus. cun - - cta stri - - cte
tu - rus. cun - - cta stri - cte
tu - rus. cun - - cta stri - - cte
tu - rus. cun - - cta stri - - cte

39
R
dis - - cus - - - su - rus
Di - es
dis - - cus - - - su - rus
Di - es
dis - - cus - - - su - rus
Di - es
dis - - cus - - - su - rus. Quantus tre - mor est fu - tu-rus.
R
sf
43
i - rae, di - es il - la,
di - es
i - rae, di - es il - la,
di - es
i - rae, di - es il - la.
di - es
quantus tre - mor est fu - tu-rus
sf
47
S
i- - rae, di - es il - la,
quan - tus
i- - rae, di - es il - la,
quan - tus
i- - rae, di - es il - la,
quan - tus
quantus tre - mor est fu - tu - rus, quan - tus
S
sf

51
tre - mor est fu - tu - rus, quan-do ju - dex est ven -
tre - mor est fu - tu - rus, quan-do ju - dex est ven -
tre - mor est fu - tu - rus, quan-do ju - dex est ven -
tre - mor est fu - tu - rus, quan-do ju - dex est ven -
54
tu - rus, cuncta stri - cte dis - cus - su - rus.
tu - rus, cuncta stri - cte dis - cus - su - rus.
tu - rus, cuncta stri - cte dis - cus - su - rus.
tu - rus, cuncta stri - cte dis - cus - su - rus.
57
T
cun - cta stri - cte, stri - cte
cun - cta stri - cte, stri - cte
cun - cta stri - cte, stri - cte
cun - cta stri - cte, stri - cte
T

60
dis - cus - su - - - rus, cun - - - cta stri - cte,
dis - cus - su - - - rus, cun - - - cta stri - cte,
dis - cus - su - - - rus, cun - - - cta
dis - cus su - - - rus, cun - - cta
63
stri - cte dis - cus - su - -- rus.
stri - cte dis - cus - su - - - rus.
stri - cte, stri - cte dis - cus - su - - - rus.
stri - cte, stri - cte dis - cus - su - - - rus.
66

## TEXT AND TRANSLATION

| | |
|---|---|
| Kyrie eleison,<br>Kyrie eleison,<br>Christe eleison. | Lord, have mercy,<br>Christ, have mercy,<br>Lord, have mercy. |
| Dies ire, dies illa,<br>solvet saeclum in favilla,<br>teste David cum Sybilla. | Day of wrath, a day when<br>The world will dissolve in ashes,<br>As foretold by David and the Sibyl. |
| Quantus tremor est futurus,<br>Judex est venturus,<br>Cuncta stricte discussurus. | What trembling there will be<br>When the judge comes<br>To adjudicate all things strictly. |

## Wolfgang Amadeus Mozart

String Quartet in D Minor, K. 421, first and third movements

This quartet, composed in 1783, is part of a set of six quartets that Mozart published together and dedicated to Haydn. During Mozart's lifetime, Haydn's quartets were widely admired; in his "Haydn Quartets," Mozart takes inspiration from the older composer. (For an example of a Haydn quartet movement, see p. 199.)

From *Wolfgang Amadeus Mozart: Complete String Quartets*. New York: Dover Publications, Inc.

25
p
p
cresc.
cresc.
29
p
p
p
f
f
f
p
sf
p
p sf p
33
p
sf
p
p
sf
p
sf
p
sf
p
tr
37
tr
tr
tr
40
1.
cresc.
cresc.
cresc.
cresc.
2.
cresc.
cresc.
cresc.
cresc.
f
f
f
f

43
50
59
63
67
p
pp
f
fp
cresc.

70
sotto voce
sotto voce
77
83
cresc.
cresc.
cresc.
cresc.
89
95
cresc.
cresc.

99
102
107
110
113
1.
2.
cresc.
tr

MENUETTO. (Allegretto.)
Violin 1
Violin 2
Viola
Cello
f
12
p
cresc.
24
pp
36
Trio.
sempre p
pizz.

45
55
arco
Menuetto D.C.

## Wolfgang Amadeus Mozart

*Variations on "Ah, vous dirai-je Maman"*

Mozart composed this theme and variations early in the 1780s. The theme is a French folk song, "Ah, vous dirai-je Maman," the same tune as "Twinkle, Twinkle, Little Star." Because this tune is so familiar, it makes this sectional variation set an ideal vehicle for studying variation technique.

From *Mozart Masterpieces for Solo Piano*. New York: Dover Publications, Inc.

49
VAR. II.
legato
55
61
tr
67
73
VAR. III.
3
81
f
89

97
VAR. IV.
3
3
103
109
115
121
VAR. V.
p
129

138
145
VAR. VI.
p
legato
cresc.
149
f
p legato
154
cresc.
159
f
p
cresc.
164
f

169
VAR. VII.
f
174
181
f
f
187
VAR. VIII.
Minore.
193
p
f
201
p
210
f

217
VAR. IX.
Maggiore.
p
f
p
229
p
f
241
VAR. X.
L. H.
p
f
245
L.H.
p
250
f
254
L.H.
p
259
f

VAR. XI.
Adagio.
p
fp
cresc.
VAR. XII.
Allegro.
f
tr

297
301
305
tr
309
1.
312
2.
316
320

## Krzysztof Penderecki (b. 1933)

*Threnody for the Victims of Hiroshima*
(to rehearsal 25)

The *Threnody*, composed in 1960, with its evocative title and striking sonic character, brought Polish composer Krzysztof Penderecki international recognition. The piece is significant for its graphic notation, invented by Penderecki and employed in many of his later compositions. Though he initially gave it a generic title, after hearing a performance of the work, Penderecki renamed it to memorialize the victims of the world's first atomic bomb.

### ABBREVIATIONS AND SYMBOLS

Sharpen a quarter-tone.

Sharpen three quarter-tones.

Flatten a quarter-tone.

Flatten three quarter-tones.

Highest note of the instrument (no definite pitch). ▲

Play between bridge and tailpiece.

Arpeggio on 4 strings behind the bridge.

Play on the tailpiece (arco) by bowing the tailpiece at an angle of 90∞ to its longer axis.

Molto vibrato.

Very slow vibrato with a ¼ tone frequency difference produced by sliding the finger.

Very rapid non-rhythmisized tremolo.

| | |
|---|---|
| ordinario | ord. |
| sul ponticello | s. p. |
| sul tasto | s. t. |
| col legno | c. l. |
| legno battuto | l. batt. |

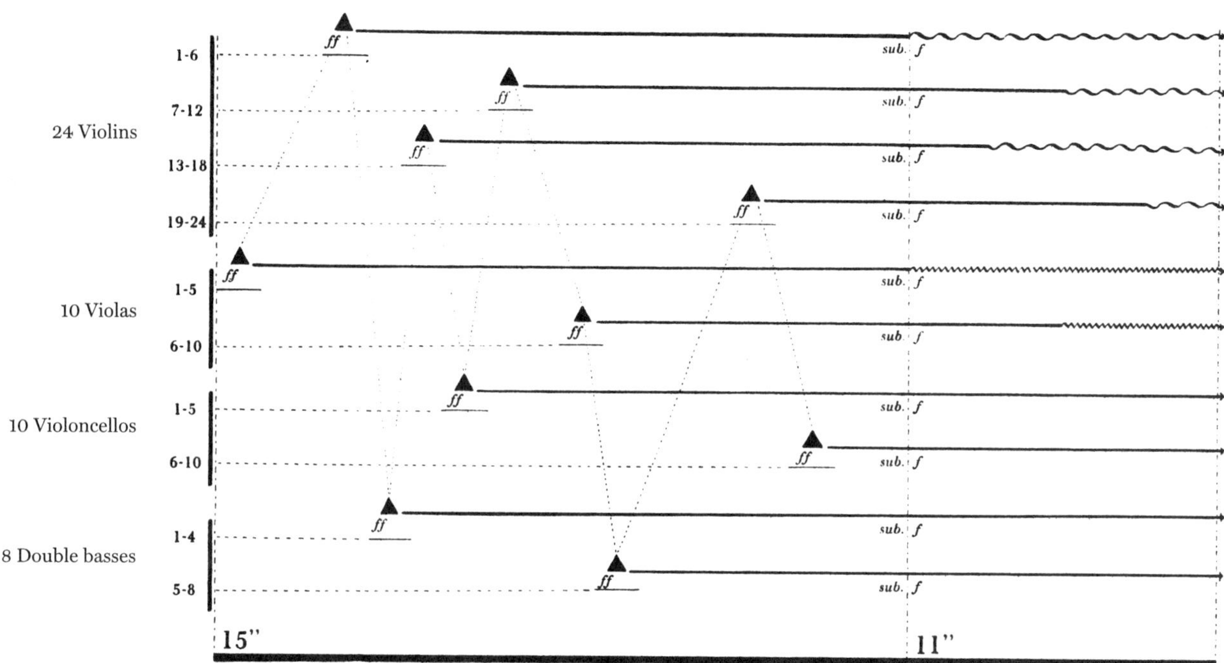
24 Violins
1-6
7-12
13-18
19-24
10 Violas
1-5
6-10
10 Violoncellos
1-5
6-10
8 Double basses
1-4
5-8
ff
sub. f
15"
11"

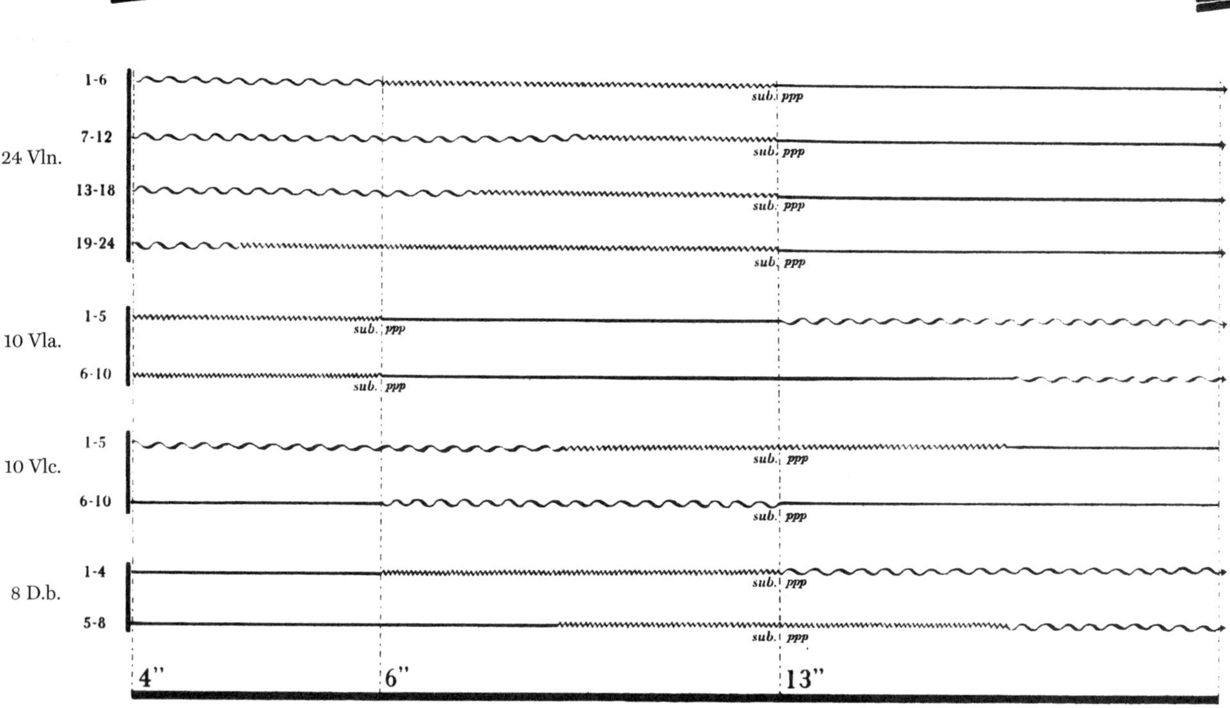
24 Vln.
1-6
7-12
13-18
19-24
10 Vla.
1-5
6-10
10 Vlc.
1-5
6-10
8 D.b.
1-4
5-8
sub. ppp
4"
6"
13"

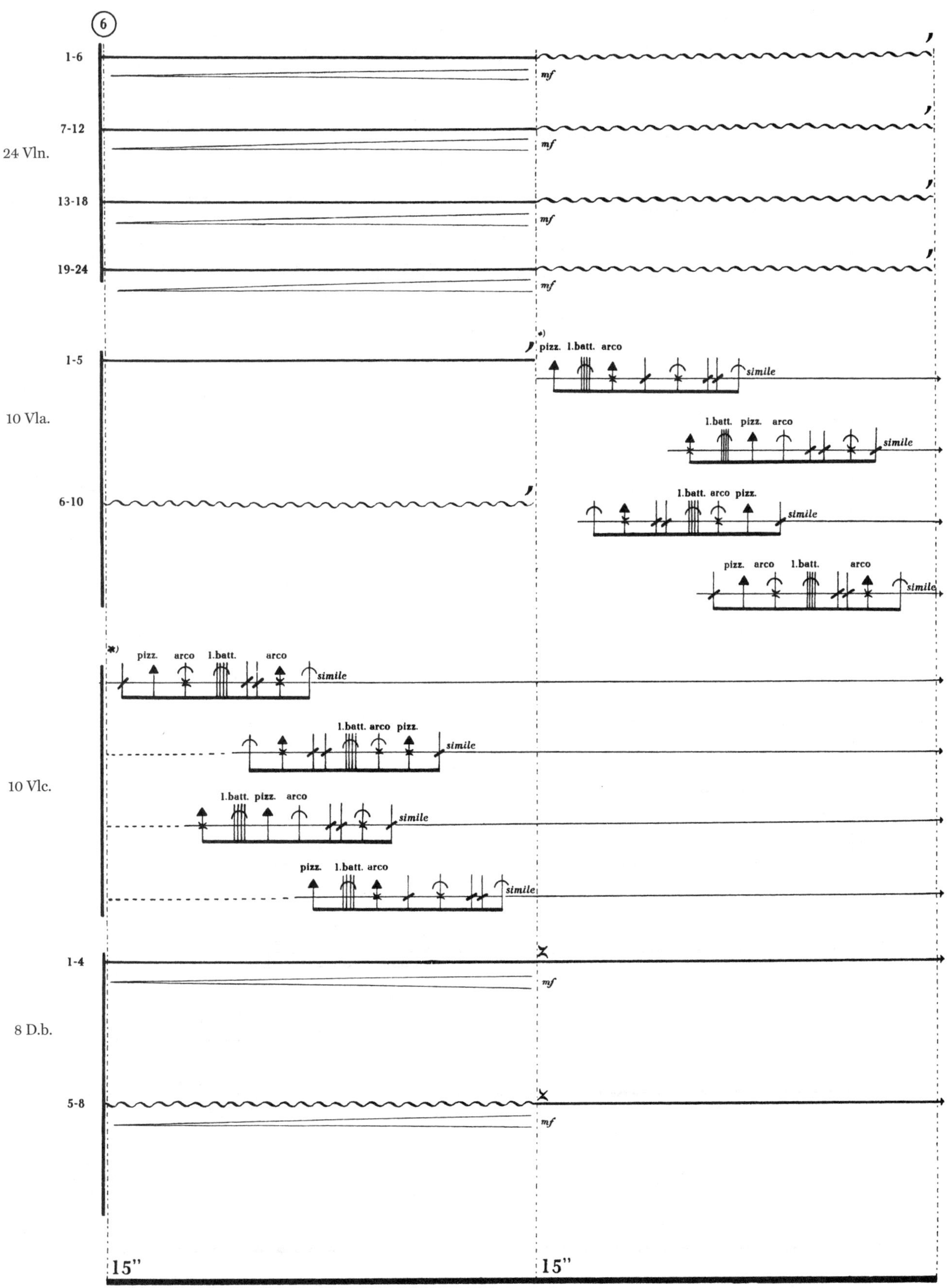


*Each instrumentalist chooses one of the four given groups and executes it (within a fixed space of time) as rapidly as possible.

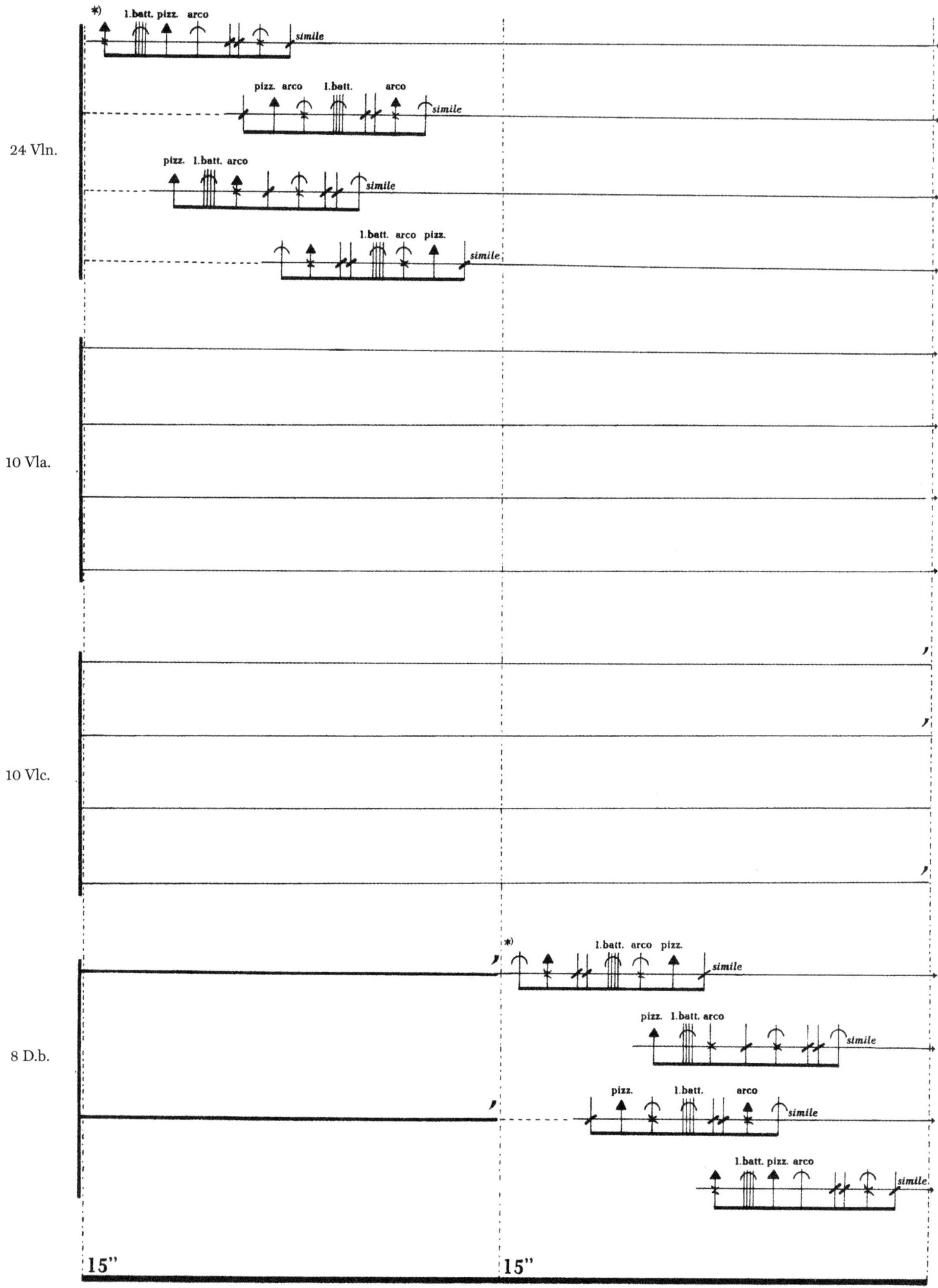
*)
l.batt. pizz. arco
simile
pizz. arco l.batt. arco
simile
24 Vln.
pizz. l.batt. arco
simile
l.batt. arco pizz.
simile
10 Vla.
10 Vlc.
*)
l.batt. arco pizz.
simile
pizz. l.batt. arco
simile
8 D.b.
pizz. l.batt. arco
simile
l.batt. pizz. arco
simile
15"
15"

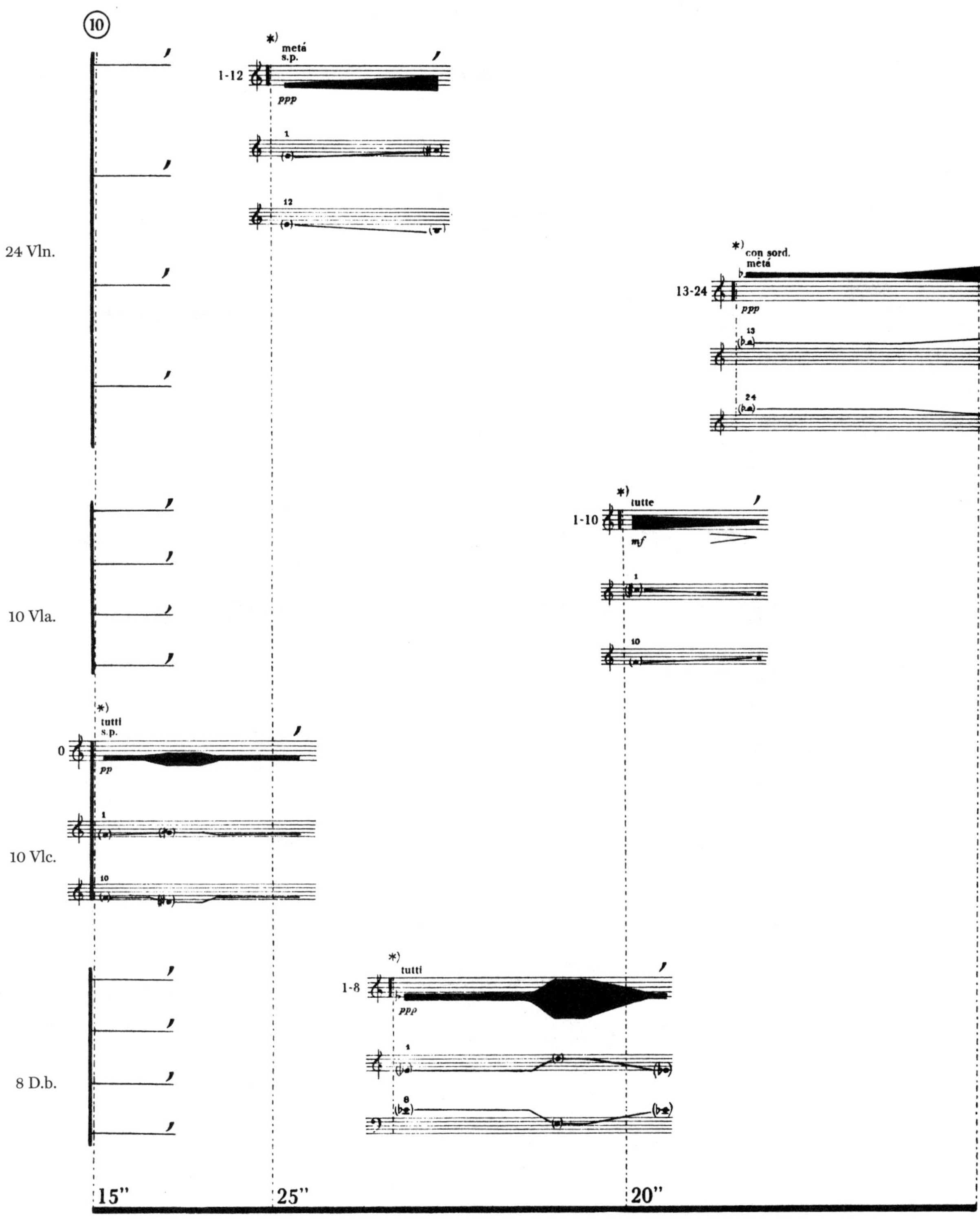


*Exact notation is given in the parts.

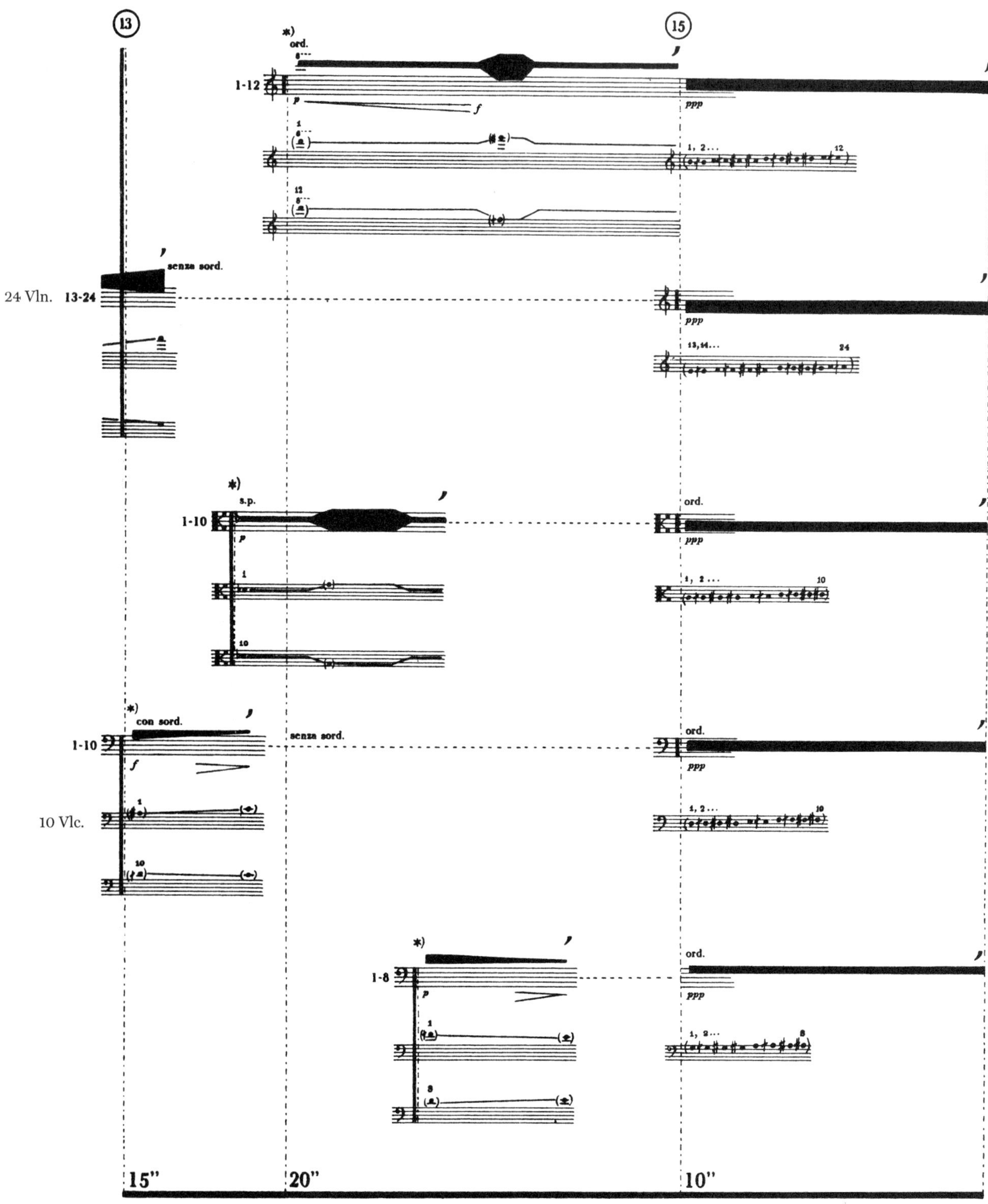
13
15
ord.
1-12
p
f
ppp
24 Vln. 13-24
senza sord.
s.p.
1-10
ord.
con sord.
senza sord.
10 Vlc.
1-8
15"
20"
10"

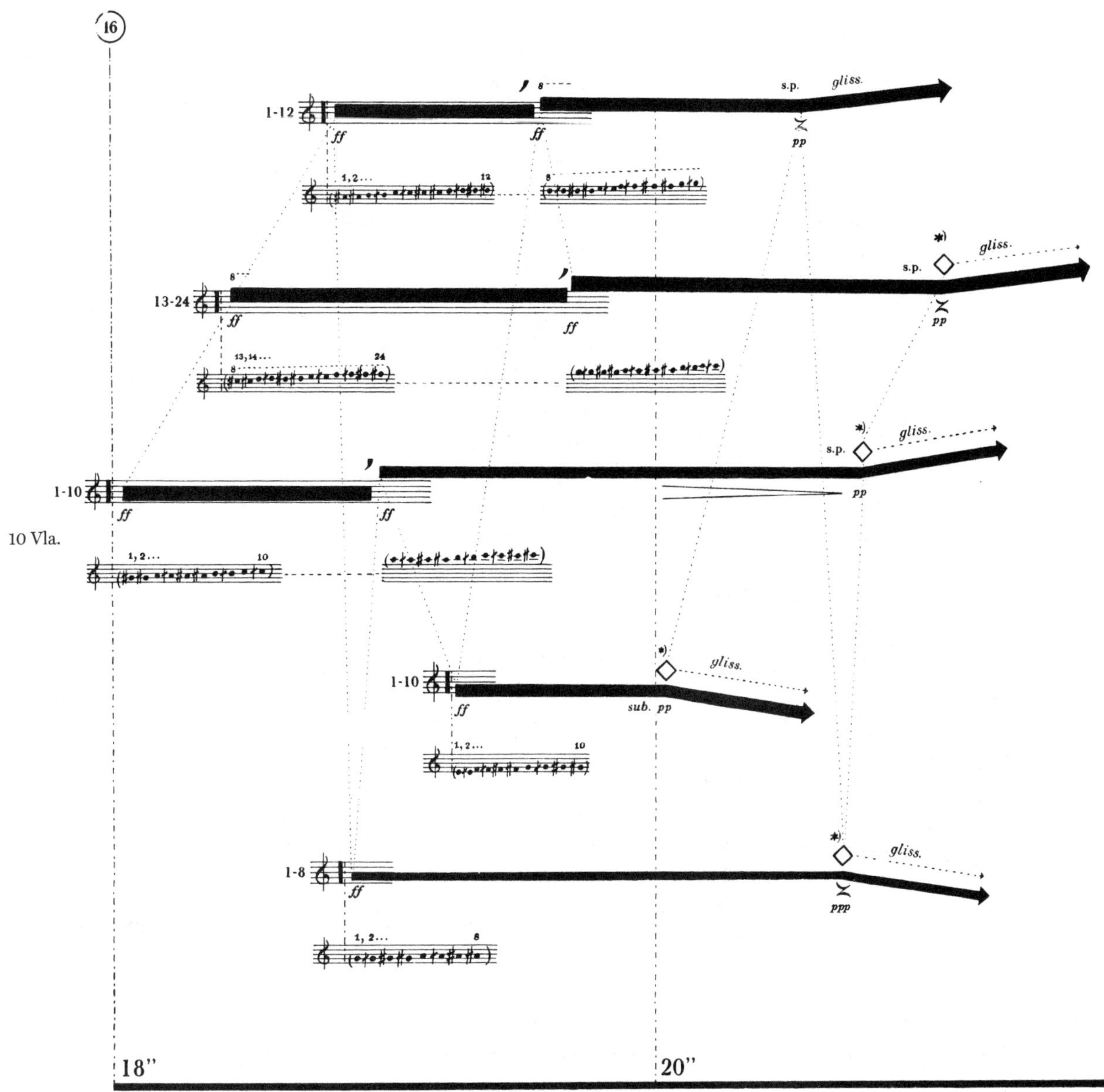


*Flageolet tones.

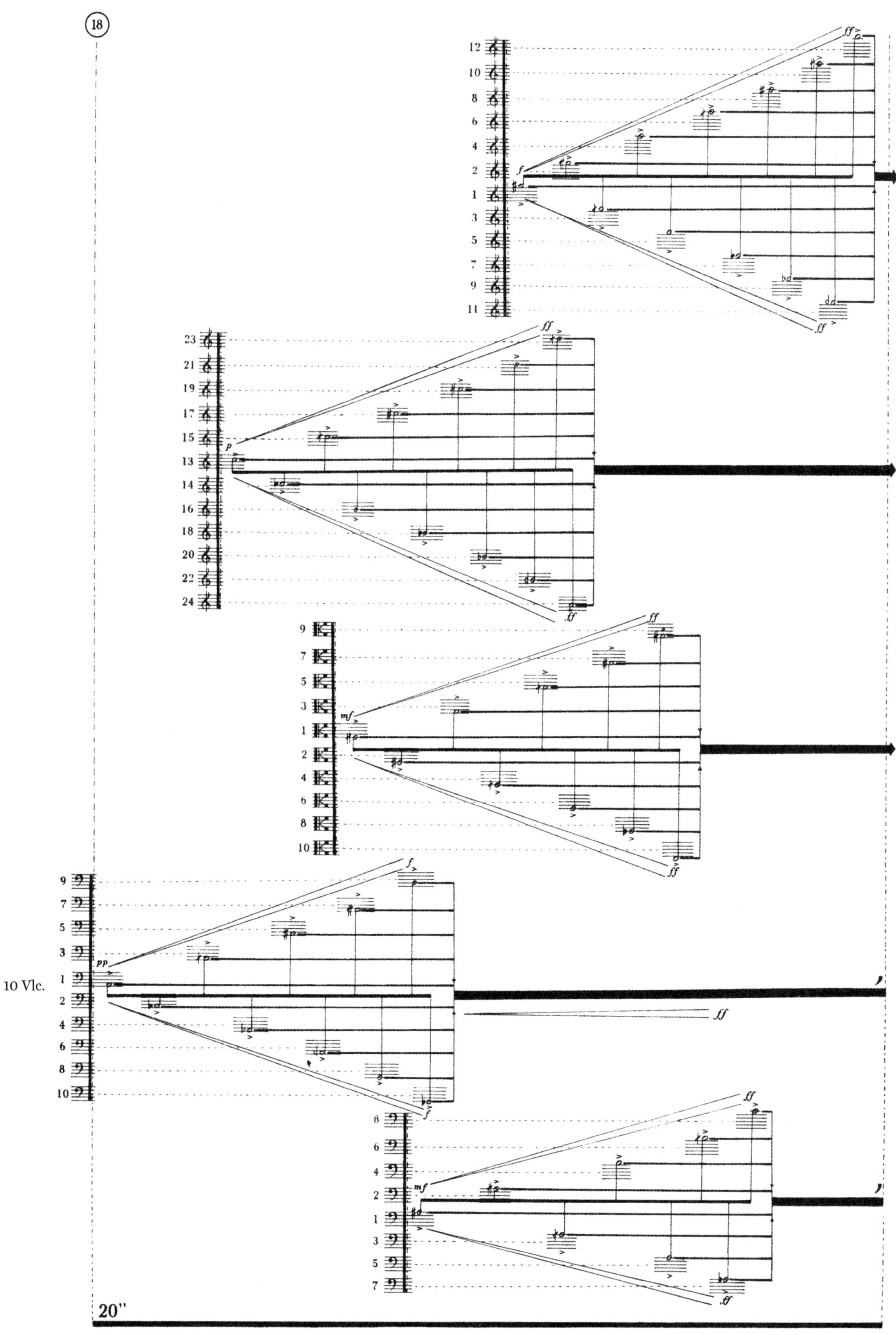
18
12
10
8
6
4
2
1
3
5
7
9
11
23
21
19
17
15
13
14
16
18
20
22
24
9
7
5
3
1
2
4
6
8
10
10 Vlc.
9
7
5
3
1
2
4
6
8
10
8
6
4
2
1
3
5
7
20"

19

12 Vln. 1-12

12 Vln. 13-24

10 Vla. 1-10

20

10 Vlc. 1-10 *gliss.* *fff* *f*

1, 2... 10 1, 2... 10

8 D.b. 1-8 *gliss.* *fff* *f*

1, 2... 8 1, 2... 8

15" 7" 5"

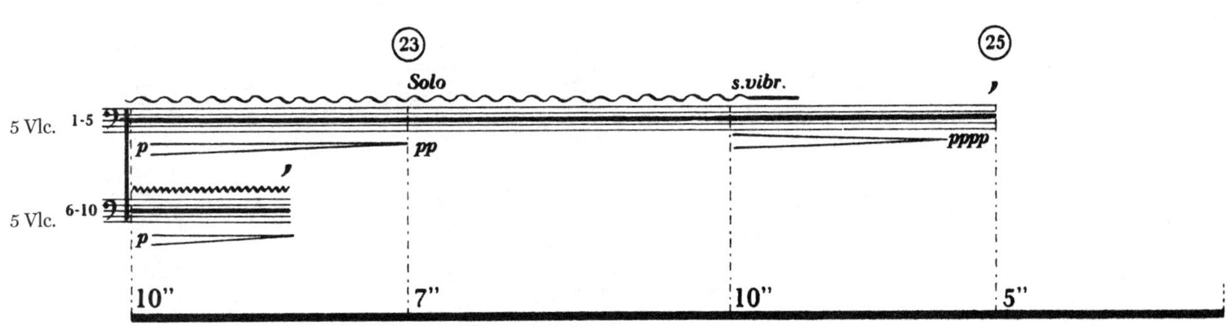

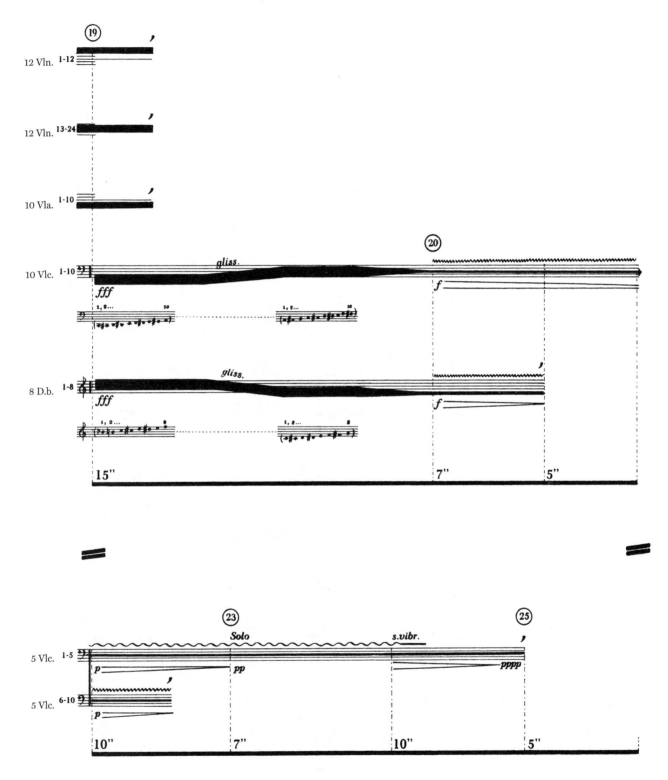

## **Henry Purcell (1659–1695)**

From *Dido and Aeneas*

*Dido and Aeneas,* composed in 1689, is based on a passage from Virgil's *Aenead.* In the opera, the Trojan prince, Aeneas, and Dido, queen of Carthage, fall in love; yet a sorceress tricks Aeneas into abandoning Dido, leading to her demise. In "Ah, Belinda, I am prest," the first aria of the opera, Dido reflects on her initial anguish at being pursued by Aeneas. In "When I am laid in earth," Dido, heartbroken at her abandonment by Aeneas, prepares for death. Both arias are written above a ground bass.

### "Ah, Belinda, I am prest" (aria)

Libretto by Nahum Tate

From *Henry Purcell: Dido and Aeneas: An Opera.* New York: Broude Brothers, n.d.

22
I — am prest with — tor - ment, Ah, ah, ah, Be - lin - da, I — am
30
prest — with tor - ment not to be con - fest, Peace and I are
36
stran - gers grown, Peace and I are stran - gers, stran - gers grown. I
45
lan - - - guish till my grief is known, I lan - - - - - - - - guish, I

53
lan - guish till my grief — is known, Yet would not, yet would not, would — not
59
have — it — guess'd. Peace and I are
66
stran - gers grown, Peace and I are stran - gers, stran - gers
72
grown.

## "Thy hand, Belinda" (recitative) and "When I am laid in earth" (aria)

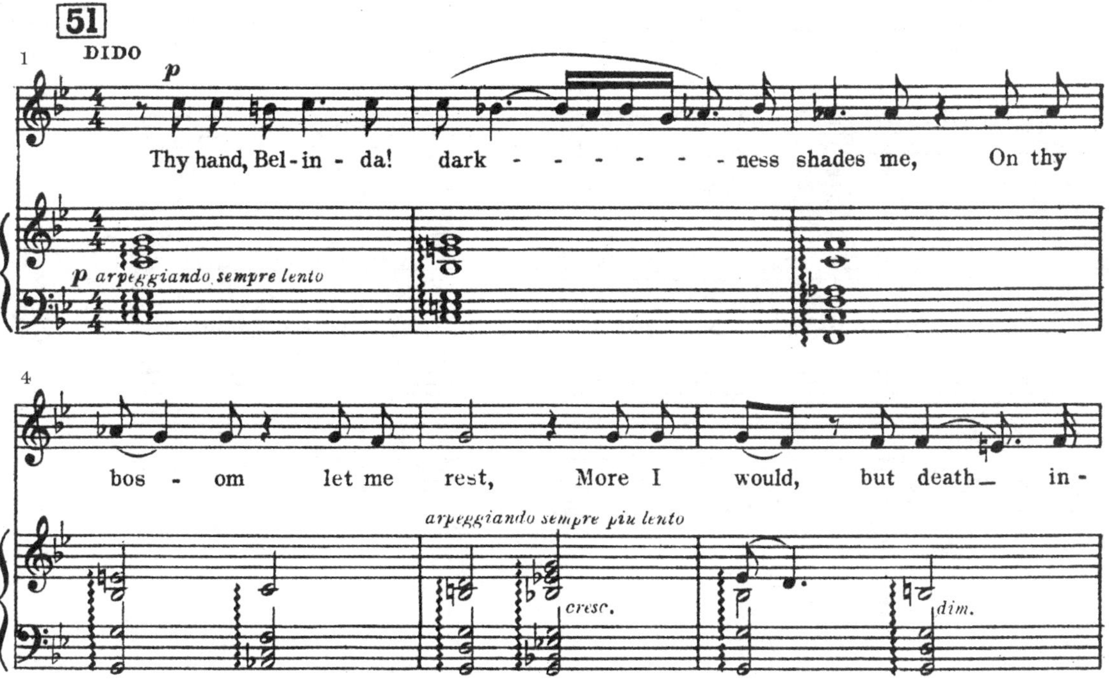

7
-vades me Death is now a wel - come guest.
pp
11
52
When I am laid, am laid in
pp
17
earth, may my wrongs cre - ate no trou - ble, no trou - ble in thy
22
breast. When I am laid, am laid in earth, may my

28
wrongs cre - ate no trou - ble, no trouble in thy breast. Re-
34
- mem-ber me, re - mem-ber me, But ah! forget my
40
fate, Re - member me, but ah! for - get my fate Re -
53
45
- member me, re - member me, But ah! forget my

50
fate, Re - mem-ber me, but ah! ______ for - get my fate!
p
cresc.
56
f
diminuendo sempre
pp

## Henry Purcell

"Music for a While"

Purcell wrote "Music for a While" in 1692, to be performed as incidental music for John Dryden and Nathaniel Lee's English adaptation of the ancient Greek tragedy *Oedipus Rex*. Many of Purcell's works were originally composed for the theater. The text refers to Alecto, one of the Furies, who were often depicted with wings and with their heads wreathed with serpents. Two recordings contrast a modern piano arrangement with a Baroque-style continuo accompaniment.

Arranged by Michael Tippett and Walter Bergmann

6
while shall all your cares be - guile, shall all, all, all, shall all, shall
9
all, shall all your cares be - guile: Won - d'ring, won -
12
- d'ring how your pains were eas'd, eas'd, eas'd And dis -
15
dain - ing to be pleas'd Till A - lec - to free the

17
dead, till A-lec - - - - - to free the dead from
(pp)
19
their e-ter - - - - nal, e-ter - - - - - - - nal
22
bands,
Till the snakes drop, drop, drop, drop, drop,
(p)
(pp)
25
drop, drop, drop, drop from her head. And the

27
whip, and the whip from out her_ hands.
(p)
29
Mu - sic, mu - sic for a_ while shall all your cares be-
(pp)
32
guile,_ shall all, all, all, shall all, all,
34
all,_ shall all_ your cares be - guile, all, all, all,

36
all, all, all, all, all, shall all_ your cares be - guile.

## Maurice Ravel (1875–1937)

"Aoua!," from *Chansons madécasses,* for flute, cello, piano, and soprano

"Aoua!" is one of three songs that comprise the *Chansons madécasses* (*Songs of Madagascar*), composed in 1925–26 for Elizabeth Sprague Coolidge, an American pianist and patron of chamber music. Ravel's songs are settings of poems about the island of Madagascar by Évariste de Parny, and "Aoua!" describes the fates of European colonists who attempted to enslave the Madagascans. The song poignantly mixes the languid exoticism of the foreign locale with the stirring cries of an oppressed people.

Text by Évariste de Parny

4
Sordina.arco
pp
.tans du ri.va. - - ge.
8
1
pp
8
p
Du tems de nos pè.res, des blancs descen . di.rent dans cette î . le; on leur dit: Voi.là des
12
ter . res; que vos fem . mes les cul.ti . vent. Soy.ez jus.tes, soy.ez bons, et de.ve.nez nos frè .

16
-res.
Les blancs pro - mirent, et ce - pendant ils fai -
2
8b
8
20
senza Sordina
poco crescendo
-saient des retranchemens. Un fort me-na-çant s'é-le-va; le tonner-re fut renfermé
3
8
8
8
24
crescendo e accelerando poco a poco
dans des bouches d'airain; leurs prê - tres vou - lu-rent nous don-ner un Dieu
3

27
— que nous ne connaissons pas; ils par-lè-rent en-fin d'o-bé-is-san-ce et d'escla-
30
FLAUTO
mf
cresc.
sempre cresc.
-va- - - -ge: plu-tôt la mort! Le car-na-ge fut long et ter-
3
♩=76
sempre cresc.
8
32
-ri-ble; mais, mal-gré la fou-dre qu'ils vo-mis-saient, et qui é-cra-sait des armées en-
8

34
ff
pizz.
ff
ff
-tières, ils furent tous extermi - nés. Aoua!
Aoua!
ff
8
37
Allegro feroce
Quasi tromba
ff
Allegro feroce
Mé-fi-ez-vous des blancs!
4
Allegro feroce ♩=168
f
Ped.
42
Nous a - vons vu de nouveaux ty - rans, plus forts et plus nom - breux, plan -

47
-ter leur pa-vil - lon sur— le ri - va - ge: le
51
ciel a com-bat - tu pour— nous; il a fait tom - ber sur— eux
55
les— pluies, les tem - pê-tes et les vents em - poi-sonnés.
tr
sf
sf

59
Molto ritenuto
Ils ne sont plus, et nous vi - vons, et nous vi-vons li - bres.
Molto ritenuto
63
Adagio
pp
Aoua!
Aoua!
Méfi-ez-vous des blancs, habitans du ri-
5
Adagio
pp
67
Sord.
p espressivo
Sordina
arco
p
I
II
-va - - - - ge.
ppp

## TEXT AND TRANSLATION

"Aoua!"

Aoua! Aoua! Méfiez-vous des blancs,
Habitants du rivage.
Du temps de nos pères,
Des blancs descendirent dans cette île.
On leur dit: Voilà des terres,
Que vos femmes les cultivent.
Soyez justes, soyez bons,
Et devenez nos frères.

Les blancs promirent, et cependant
Ils faisaient des retranchements.
Un fort menaçant s'éleva;
Le tonnerre fut renfermé
Dans des bouches d'airain;
Leurs prêtres voulurent nous donner
Un Dieu que nous ne connaissons pas,
Ils parlèrent enfin
D'obéissance et d'esclavage.

Plutôt la mort!
Le carnage fut long et terrible;
Mais, malgré la foudre qu'ils vormissaient,
Et qui écrasait des armées entières,
Ils furent tous exterminés.

Aoua! Aoua! Méfiez-vous des blancs!

Nous avons vu de nouveaux tyrans,
Plus forts et plus nombreaux,
Planter leur pavillon sur le rivage:
Le ciel a combattu pour nous;
Il a fait tomber sur eux les pluies,
Les tempêtes et les vents empoisonnés.
Ils ne sont plus, et nous vivons,
Et nous vivons libres.

Aoua! Méfiez-vous des blancs,
Habitants du rivage.

"Aoua!"

Aoua! Aoua! Beware of the white men,
Inhabitants of the shore.
In the times of our fathers,
The white men descended to this island.
They said to them: "Here is some land
That your women may cultivate.
Be fair, be good,
And become our brothers."

The white men promised, and yet
They were making entrenchments.
A menacing fort rose up,
The thunder was confined
In the mouths of cannons.
Their priests wanted to give us
A God that we did not know.
Finally, they spoke
Of obedience and slavery.

Rather death!
The carnage was long and terrible,
But despite the lightning that they vomited,
Which crushed entire armies,
They were all exterminated.

Aoua! Aoua! Beware of the white men!

We saw new tyrants,
Stronger and more numerous,
Planting their flag on the shore.
Heaven fought for us;
It made rain fall on them,
Storms and poisoned winds.
They are no more, and we live,
And we live free.

Aoua! Aoua! Beware of the white men,
Inhabitants of the shore.

## Steve Reich (b. 1936)

*Piano Phase* (patterns 1–32)

Reich composed *Piano Phase* in 1967. Like many of his early works, the composition received its premiere at an art gallery: the Park Place Gallery in New York, known for sponsoring performances of modern music. Because of its extended repetition of a simple melodic idea, *Piano Phase* is an example of the artistic movement that came to be known as minimalism. In this work, the two pianos begin together, then Piano II accelerates until it is one sixteenth note ahead. Listen for the pianos to move out of phase, then lock in on the new alignment of the patterns.

♩. = ca. 72

Repeat each bar approximately number of times written.

*hold tempo 1*

** The piece may be played an octave lower than written, when played on marimbas.*

*a.v.s. = accelerando very slightly.*

13 (x 12 - 24)
(x 4 - 16)
14 (x 4 - 8)
15 (x 4 - 8)
(tempo 1)
hold tempo 1
a.v.s.
hold tempo 1
fade
out
16 (x 6 - 8)
17 (x 16 - 32)
(x 6 - 18)
18 (x 16 - 32)
(x 6 - 18)
19 (x 16 - 32)
(x 6 - 18)
(tempo 1)
(tempo 1)
(tempo 1)
a.v.s
hold tempo 1
a.v.s.
hold tempo 1
a.v.s.
fade in
mf
20 (x 16 - 32)
(x 6 - 18)
21 (x 16 - 32)
(x 6 - 18)
22 (x 16 - 32)
(x 6 - 18)
23 (x 16 - 32)
(x 6 - 18)
(tempo 1)
(tempo 1)
(tempo 1)
(tempo 1)
hold tempo 1
a.v.s.
hold tempo 1
a.v.s.
hold tempo 1
a.v.s.
hold tempo 1
a.v.s.
24 (x 16 - 32)
x 6 - 18
25 (x 8 - 24)
26 (x 8 - 16)
26a
27 (x 8 - 24)
(tempo 1)
fade
out
p
a.v.s.
hold tempo 1
hold tempo 1
28 (x 24 - 48)
(x 16 - 32)
29 (x 48 - 60)
(x 16 - 32)
30 (x 48 - 60)
(x 16 - 32)
31 (x 48 - 60)
(x 16 - 32)
32 (x 24 - 48)
fade in
mf
(tempo 1)
(tempo 1)
(tempo 1)
(tempo 1)
Cue for end (see notes)
a.v.s.
hold tempo 1
a.v.s.
hold tempo 1
a.v.s.
hold tempo 1
a.v.s.
hold tempo 1
1967

## Domenico Scarlatti (1685–1757)

Sonata in G Major, L. 388

Scarlatti published this sonata in 1738, as a part of a collection of *Essercizi* ("Exercises") for harpsichord that was dedicated to his patron, João V, King of Portugal. Scarlatti's sonatas differ from Classical-era sonatas in that they consist of a single movement in binary form.

38
tr
tr
45
tr
52
59
66
72

## Arnold Schoenberg (1874–1951)

*Klavierstück,* Op. 33a

Schoenberg composed this *Klavierstück* in 1929 for an anthology of twentieth-century piano music published by Universal Edition. The piece exemplifies Schoenberg's use of serialism, a compositional technique he developed in the 1920s, while retaining some aspects of sonata form.

Used by permission of Belmont Music Publishers.

a tempo
10
mf
poco rit
molto rit
12
fp
p dolce
f
Ped
a tempo
14
cantabile
p
16
p cantabile

heftiger
poco rit
19
f martellato
Ped.
ruhiger
cantabile
21
p
rit
a tempo
23
p
dolce
f energisch
ff
p
26
steigernd
scherzando
sf
p martellato

28
f
f
29
8
30
f
31
mp
5
4

32
ff
p
rit
Ruhig
34
p dolce
36
steigernd
p cresc.
38
rit
f
ff

## Franz Schubert (1797–1828)

From *Die schöne Müllerin*

These songs are part of the song cycle *Die schöne Müllerin* published in 1823. The poems set by Schubert for both this cycle and *Winterreise* (p. 352) are by Wilhelm Müller. Here their subject is the unrequited love of a transient young miller for the mill owner's daughter.

### "Der Neugierige"

Text by Wilhelm Müller

From *Franz Schubert: Complete Song Cycles*. New York: Dover Publications, Inc.

18
fra_gen, ob_ mich mein Herz be_log.
O
23
Sehr langsam.
Bäch - lein mei_ner Lie - be, wie bist du heut' so
pp
26
stumm! Will ja nur Ei_nes wis - sen, ein Wört_chen um und_
30
um, ein Wörtchen um und_ um.
Ja, heisst das ei_ne
34
Wörtchen, das an_dre heisset Nein, die bei_den Wört_chen schlie_ssen die
cresc.

37
gan - ze Welt mir ein, die bei - den Wört - chen schlie - ssen die
p
cresc.
40
gan - ze Welt mir ein. O
p
pp
43
Bäch - lein mei - ner Lie - be, was bist du wun - der-
3
46
lich! Will's ja nicht wei - ter sa - gen, sag'
49
Bäch - lein, liebt sie mich? sag' Bäch - lein, liebt sie

## TEXT AND TRANSLATION

"Der Neugierige," from *Die schöne Müllerin*

Ich frage keine Blume,
Ich frage keinen Stern,
Sie können mir alle nicht sagen,
Was ich erführ' so gern.

Ich bin ja auch kein Gärtner,
Die Sterne steh'n zu hoch;
Mein Bächlein will ich fragen,
Ob mich mein Herz belog.

O Bächlein meiner Liebe,
Wie bist du heut' so stumm!
Will ja nur Eines wissen,
Ein Wörtchen um und um.

Ja, heißt das eine Wörtchen,
Das andre heißet Nein,
Die beiden Wörtchen
Schließen die ganze Welt mir ein.

O Bächlein meiner Liebe,
Was bist du wunderlich!
Will's ja nicht weiter sagen,
Sag' Bächlein, liebt sie mich?

"The Inquisitive One," from *The Fair Maid of the Mill*

I ask no flower,
I ask no star,
They cannot tell me,
What I want to know so much.

I am, anyway, no gardener,
The stars are up too high,
My brooklet I will ask
Whether my heart deceived me.

O brooklet of my love,
Why are you today so silent!
I want to know only one thing,
One little word over and over.

"Yes" is the one little word,
The other is "No";
These two little words
Comprise the whole world to me.

O brooklet of my love,
How strange you are!
I will not repeat it,
Speak, brooklet, does she love me?

# "Morgengruß"

Text by Wilhelm Müller

**Mässig.**

**Singstimme.**

**Pianoforte.**

Guten Mor - gen, schö - ne
O lass mich nur von
Ihr schlummer - trunk'nen
Nun schüt - telt ab der

6

Mül - le - rin! wo steckst du gleich das Köpfchen hin, als wär' dir was ge - sche - hen? Ver-
fer - ne steh'n, nach dei - nem lie - ben Fen - ster seh'n, von fer - ne, ganz von fer - ne! Du
Äu - ge - lein, ihr thau - be - trüb - ten Blü - me - lein, was scheu - et ihr die Son - ne? Hat
Träu - me Flor, und hebt euch frisch und frei em - por in Got - tes hel - len Mor - gen! Die

12

driesst dich denn mein Gruss so schwer? ver - stört dich denn mein Blick so sehr? So muss ich wieder
blon - des Köpfchen komm hervor, her - vor aus eu - rem run - den Thor ihr blau - en Morgen-
es die Nacht so gut gemeint, dass ihr euch schliesst und bückt und weint nach ih - rer stillen
Ler - che wir - belt in der Luft, und aus dem tie - fen Her - zen ruft die Lie - be Leid und

17

ge - hen, so muss ich wie - der ge - hen, wie - der ge - hen.
ster - ne, ihr blau - en Mor - gen - ster - ne, ihr Morgen - ster - ne!
Won - ne, nach ih - rer stil - len Won - ne, nach ih - rer Won - ne?
Sor - gen, die Lie - be Leid und Sor - gen, Leid und Sor - gen.

## TEXT AND TRANSLATION

"Morgengruß"

Guten Morgen, schöne Müllerin!
Wo steckst du gleich das Köpfchen hin,
Als wär' dir was geschehen?
Verdrießt dich denn mein Gruß so schwer?
Verstört dich denn mein Blick so sehr?
So muß ich wieder gehen.

O laß mich nur von ferne steh'n,
Nach deinem lieben Fenster seh'n,
Von ferne, ganz von ferne!
Du blondes Köpfchen, komm hervor!
Hervor aus eurem runden Tor,
Ihr blauen Morgensterne!

Ihr schlummertrunk'nen Äugelein,
Ihr taubetrübten Blümelein,
Was scheuet ihr die Sonne?
Hat es die Nacht so gut gemeint,
Daß ihr euch schließt und bückt und weint
Nach ihrer stillen Wonne?

Nun schüttelt ab der Träume Flor,
Und hebt euch frisch und frei empor
In Gottes hellen Morgen!
Die Lerche wirbelt in der Luft,
Und aus dem tiefen Herzen ruft
Die Liebe Leid und Sorgen.

"Morning Greeting"

Good morning, beautiful millermaid!
Why did you immediately hide your little head
As if something had happened to you?
Does my greeting irritate you so much?
Does my gaze upset you so much?
Then I must go again.

Oh let me just stand from afar,
Looking at your dear window,
From afar, completely from afar!
You little blond head, come out!
Out from your round gate,
You blue morning stars!

You slumber-drunk little eyes,
You dew-saddened little flowers,
Why do you shun the sun?
Has the night been so good to you
That you close up and bend over and cry
For its quiet bliss?

Now shake off the veil of dreams
And rise up fresh and free
In God's bright morning!
The skylark warbles in the air;
And from the depths of the heart calls
The pain of love and worry.

## Franz Schubert

"Du bist die Ruh"

"Du bist die Ruh," composed in 1823, is a setting of a poem by Frederich Rückert. Schubert was not the only composer inspired by this poem; Fanny Hensel also set it. (For other works by Fanny Hensel, see p. 203.)

Text by Frederich Rückert

From *Franz Schubert: Fifty-Nine Favorite Songs.* New York: Dover Publications, Inc.

24
mein Aug' und Herz.
pp
30
Kehr' ein bei mir, und schlie - sse du still hin - ter
36
dir die Pfor - ten zu. Treib' an - dern Schmerz aus die - ser
42
Brust! Voll sei dies Herz von dei - ner Lust, von dei - ner
48
Lust.

53
Dies Au - gen - zelt, von dei - nem Glanz al - lein er -
cresc.
59
hellt, o füll' es ganz, o füll' es ganz.
f
1
pp
66
Dies Au - gen - zelt, von dei - nem
cresc.
71
Glanz al - lein er - hellt, o füll' es
pp
f
1
pp
77
ganz, o füll' es ganz.

## TEXT AND TRANSLATION

"Du bist die Ruh"

Du bist die Ruh,
Der Friede mild,
Die Sehnsucht du
Und was sie stillt.

Ich weihe dir
Voll Lust und Schmerz
Zur Wohnung hier
Mein Aug' und Herz.

Kehr' ein bei mir,
Und schließe du
Still hinter dir
Die Pforten zu.

Treib' andern Schmerz
Aus dieser Brust!
Voll sei dies Herz
Von deiner Lust.

Dies Augenzelt
Von deinem Glanz
Allein erhellt,
O füll' es ganz!

"You Are Rest"

You are rest,
The gentle peace,
You are yearning
And what satiates it.

I consecrate to you,
Full of joy and pain,
As a dwelling here
My eyes and heart.

Come live with me,
And close
The gates
Quietly behind you.

Drive other pain
From this breast!
May this heart be full
Of your joy.

The tabernacle of my eyes
From your splendor
Alone is illuminated,
Oh fill it completely!

## Franz Schubert

"Erlkönig"

Schubert composed this song in 1815, when he was only eighteen years old. Goethe's poem, the text for this song, borrows the Elf King (Erlkönig) from Scandinavian mythology, where the Elf King is a spirit who haunts forests. Travelers with the misfortune of seeing or being touched by this spirit meet their death. This poem was set by many composers (including Schubert's contemporaries Carl Loewe and Johann Friedrich Reichardt), but Schubert's setting is by far the best known.

Text by Johann Wolfgang von Goethe

From *Franz Schubert: Songs to Texts by Goethe.* New York: Dover Publications, Inc.

24
Kind; er hat den Kna - ben wohl in dem Arm, er fasst ihn
30
sicher, er hält ihn warm. Mein
f
pp
37
Sohn, was birgst du so bang dein Ge-sicht? Siehst, Va - ter,
f
(pp)
43
du den Erl - kö - nig nicht? den Er - len -
mf
p
48
kö - nig mit Kron' und Schweif? Mein Sohn, es ist ein
mf

54
Ne_belstreif.
„Du lie - - bes Kind, komm,
(ppp)
60
geh mit mir! gar schö - - ne Spie - le
64
spiel' ich mit dir; manch bun - - - te Blu - men sind
68
an dem Strand; mei_ne Mut - - ter hat manch'
71
gül - - den Ge_wand".
Mein Va - ter, mein Va_ter, und hö - rest du
f

76
nicht, was Er_len_könig mir lei _ se verspricht? Sei ru_hig, bleibe
p
decresc.
82
ru_hig, mein Kind; in dür_ren Blättern säu_selt der Wind. „Willst,
87
fei _ ner__ Kna _ be, du mit mir gehn? mei_ne Töch _ ter sol _ len dich
ppp
90
war _ ten schön; mei_ne Töch _ ter__ füh _ ren den nächt _ li_chen Reihn, und
93
wie_gen und tan_zen und sin_gen dich ein, sie wie_gen und tan_zen und sin_gen dich ein".
f

97
Mein Va - ter, mein Va - ter, und siehst du nicht dort Erl -
102
kö_nigs Töchter am dü - stern Ort? Mein Sohn, mein Sohn, ich
decresc.
108
seh' es ge - nau; es scheinen die al_ten Wei - den so grau.
cresc.
ff
113
„Ich lie - be dich, mich
p
pp
118
reizt dei_ne schö_ne Ge - stalt; und bist du nicht wil - lig, so brauch' ich Ge_

123
walt". Mein Va - ter, mein Va - ter, jetzt fasst er mich an! Erl - kö - nig
fff
fz
fz
129
hat mir ein Leids ge - tan! Dem Va - ter
fz
fz
fz
fz
f
134
accelerando
grau - set's, er rei - tet geschwind, er hält in Ar - men das
cresc.
139
äch - zen - de Kind, er - reicht den
ff
fz
144
Recit.
Hof mit Müh' und Not; in seinen Armen das Kind war tot.
Andante.
fz
fp
pp
p
f

## TEXT AND TRANSLATION

"Erlkönig"

Wer reitet so spät durch Nacht und Wind?
Es ist der Vater mit seinem Kind;
Er hat den Knaben wohl in dem Arm,
Er faßt ihn sicher, er hält ihn warm.

"Mein Sohn, was birgst du so bang dein Gesicht?"
"Siehst, Vater, du den Erlkönig nicht?
Den Erlenkönig mit Kron' und Schweif?"
"Mein Sohn, es ist ein Nebelstreif."

"Du liebes Kind, komm, geh mit mir!
Gar schöne Spiele spiel ich mit dir;
Manch bunte Blumen sind an dem Strand,
Meine Mutter hat manch' gülden Gewand."

"Mein Vater, mein Vater, und hörest du nicht,
Was Erlenkönig mir leise verspricht?"
"Sei ruhig, bleibe ruhig, mein Kind;
In dürren Blättern säuselt der Wind."

"Willst, feiner Knabe, du mit mir gehn?
Meine Töchter sollen dich warten schön;
Meine Töchter führen den nächtlichen Reihn
Und wiegen und tanzen und singen dich ein."

"Mein Vater, mein Vater, und siehst du nicht dort
Erlkönigs Töchter am düstern Ort?"
"Mein Sohn, mein Sohn, ich seh es genau:
Es scheinen die alten Weiden so grau."

"Ich liebe dich, mich reizt deine schöne Gestalt;
Und bist du nicht willig, so brauch' ich Gewalt."
"Mein Vater, mein Vater, jetzt faßt er mich an!
Erlkönig hat mir ein Leids getan!"

Dem Vater grauset's, er reitet geschwind,
Er hält in Armen das ächzende Kind,
Erreicht den Hof mit Müh' und Not:
In seinen Armen das Kind war tot.

"The Elf King"

Who rides so late through night and wind?
It is the father with his child.
He has the boy secure in his arm;
He holds him safe, he keeps him warm.

"My son, why do you hide your face, so afraid?"
"Father, do you not see the Elf King?
The Elf King with crown and train?"
"My son, it is a strip of mist."

"You dear child, come away with me!
Wonderful games I will play with you;
Many colorful flowers are on the shore,
My mother has many golden garments."

"My father, my father, don't you hear
What the Elf King is quietly promising me?"
"Be still, stay calm, my child:
The wind whispers in dry leaves."

"Will you, fine boy, come with me?
My daughters shall attend to you well.
My daughters will lead their nightly round dance
And rock you and dance with you and sing to you."

"My father, my father, don't you see there
The Elf King's daughters in that dark place?"
"My son, my son, I see it clearly enough:
The old willows shine so gray."

"I love you, I am tempted by your beautiful form;
And if you are not willing, I will use force."
"My father, my father, now he has grabbed me!
The Elf King has hurt me!"

The father shudders, he rides quickly.
He holds in his arms the moaning child.
He reaches the courtyard with effort and distress;
In his arms the child was dead.

## Franz Schubert

From *Moments musicaux,* Op. 94: No. 6, in A♭ Major

In 1828, Schubert included this *Moment musical* in a collection of six brief piano pieces, together called *Moments musicaux.* Along with the Impromptus, these are among the most frequently performed of Schubert's short piano works.

From *Franz Schubert: Shorter Works for Pianoforte Solo.* New York: Dover Publications, Inc.

47
58
68
Trio.
78
87
96

Allegretto D.C.

**Franz Schubert**

Waltz in B Minor, Op. 18, No. 6

The waltz is a German dance in triple meter that enjoyed great popularity in the nineteenth century. This one belongs to a set of dance pieces Schubert composed in 1815. At parties, Schubert frequently improvised short piano waltzes, like this one, for dancing.

From *Franz Schubert: Dances for Solo Piano.* New York: Dover Publications, Inc.

## Franz Schubert

"Der Lindenbaum," from *Winterreise*

Schubert published *Winterreise,* a cycle of songs to texts by Wilhelm Müller, in 1828. Within a song cycle, a collection of songs set to the words of a single poet or poems on a general theme, the progression of individual songs may tell a story. *Winterreise* tells the story of a spurned lover who undertakes a journey in an attempt to find peace; in "Der Lindenbaum," a Linden tree evokes the lover's memories of a happy past while also hinting at an unhappy future.

Text by Wilhelm Müller

From *Franz Schubert: Complete Song Cycles.* New York: Dover Publications, Inc.

19
manches liebe Wort; es zog in Freud' und Lei_de zu ihm_mich immer fort.
fp
pp
25
3
28
Ich musst' auch heu_te wan_dern vor_bei in tie_fer Nacht, da
pp
33
hab' ich noch im Dun_kel die Au_gen zu_ge_macht. Und sei_ne Zweige
38
rausch_ten, als rie_fen sie mir zu: komm her zu mir, Ge_sel_le, hier

43
find'st du dei-ne Ruh!
Die
fz
46
kal - ten Win-de blie - sen mir grad' in's An - ge-
p
fz
p
49
sicht, der Hut flog mir vom Kop - fe, ich
cresc.
f
52
wen - de-te mich nicht.
decresc.
p
decresc.
55
fp

58
Nun bin ich manche Stun - de ent - fernt von je - nem Ort, und
ppp
pp
63
im - mer hör' ich's rau - schen: du fän - dest Ru - he dort! Nun bin ich manche
68
Stun - de ent - fernt von jenem Ort, und im - mer hör' ich's rau - schen: du
fp
73
fän - dest Ruhe dort, du fän - dest Ru - he dort!
fp
77
pp

## TEXT AND TRANSLATION

"Der Lindenbaum," from *Winterreise*

Am Brunnen vor dem Tore
Da steht ein Lindenbaum;
Ich träumt' in seinem Schatten
So manchen süßen Traum.

Ich schnitt in seine Rinde
So manches liebe Wort;
Es zog in Freud' und Leide
Zu ihm mich immer fort.

Ich mußt' auch heute wandern
Vorbei in tiefer Nacht,
Da hab' ich noch im Dunkel
Die Augen zugemacht.

Und seine Zweige rauschten,
Als riefen sie mir zu:
Komm her zu mir, Geselle,
Hier find'st du deine Ruh'!

Die kalten Winde bliesen
Mir grad' ins Angesicht;
Der Hut flog mir vom Kopfe,
Ich wendete mich nicht.

Nun bin ich manche Stunde
Entfernt von jenem Ort,
Und immer hör' ich's rauschen:
Du fändest Ruhe dort!

"The Linden Tree," from *Winter Journey*

At the well in front of the gate
There stands a linden tree.
I have dreamed in its shadows
So many sweet dreams.

I carved in its bark
So many loving words;
It drew me, in joy and sorrow,
To it always.

I had to travel by it again today
In dead of night,
I had, even in the darkness,
To close my eyes.

And its branches rustled
As if calling to me:
"Come here to me, traveler,
Here you will find your peace!"

The cold wind blew
Directly in my face,
The hat flew off my head,
I did not turn back.

Now I am many hours
Away from that place,
And still I hear the rustling:
"There you would have found peace."

## Clara Schumann (1819–1896)

"Liebst du um Schönheit"

"Liebst du um Schönheit" was published in 1841 as part of a collection of songs composed by Clara Schumann and her husband, Robert, all with texts by Friedrich Rückert. The Schumanns frequently collaborated on song composition, reading texts to one another and playing each other's music at the piano.

Text by Friedrich Rückert

13
o nicht mich lie - - be!
mf
Lie - be den Früh - ling,
der
mf
p
17
jung ist je - des Jahr!
mf
Liebst du um Schät - ze,
mf
21
o nicht mich lie - - be!
Lie - be die
24
Meer - - frau, sie hat viel Per - len klar.
rit.

27
Bewegter
f
Liebst du um Lie - be,
o ja mich lie - - be!
31
Liebst du um Lie - be,
o ja mich lie - be,
lie - be mich im - mer,
34
f
dich lieb ich im - - - mer - dar!
rit.
a tempo
37
rit.

## TEXT AND TRANSLATION

"Liebst du um Schönheit"

Liebst du um Schönheit,
O nicht mich liebe!
Liebe die Sonne,
Sie trägt ein gold'nes Haar!

Liebst du um Jugend,
O nicht mich liebe!
Liebe den Frühling,
Der jung ist jedes Jahr!

Liebst du um Schätze,
O nicht mich liebe.
Liebe die Meerfrau,
sie hat viel Perlen klar.

Liebst du um Liebe,
O ja, mich liebe!
Liebe mich immer,
Dich lieb' ich immerdar!

"If You Love for Beauty"

If you love for beauty,
Oh do not love me!
Love the sun;
She has golden hair!

If you love for youthfulness,
Oh do not love me!
Love the springtime;
It is young every year!

If you love for wealth,
Oh do not love me!
Love the mermaid;
She has many fair pearls.

If you love for love itself,
Oh yes, love me!
Love me always,
And I will love you forever!

## Robert Schumann (1810–1856)

From *Album for the Young,* Op. 68

Schumann completed his *Album for the Young,* a collection of pedagogical piano pieces, in 1848. Several of the pieces were originally written for Schumann's daughter Marie. Like the two that appear here, most of the compositions in the album have descriptive titles and are short character pieces that depict the "story" of their titles.

### No. 3: "Trällerliedchen" ("Humming Song")

From *Piano Music of Robert Schumann, Series II.* New York: Dover Publications, Inc.

# No. 8: "Wilder Reiter" ("Wild Rider")

## Robert Schumann

From *Dichterliebe*

Schumann was known for focusing his compositional energies exclusively on a single genre, such as the song or the symphony, for an extended period of time. He composed *Dichterliebe,* a song cycle to texts of Heinrich Heine, during what he called his "year of song," 1840. Over the course of this year, Schumann composed more than 160 art songs, while he waged a legal battle against his future wife's father, who had refused to allow their marriage.

### "Im wunderschönen Monat Mai"

Text by Heinrich Heine

From *Robert Schumann: Selected Songs for Voice and Piano.* New York: Dover Publications, Inc.

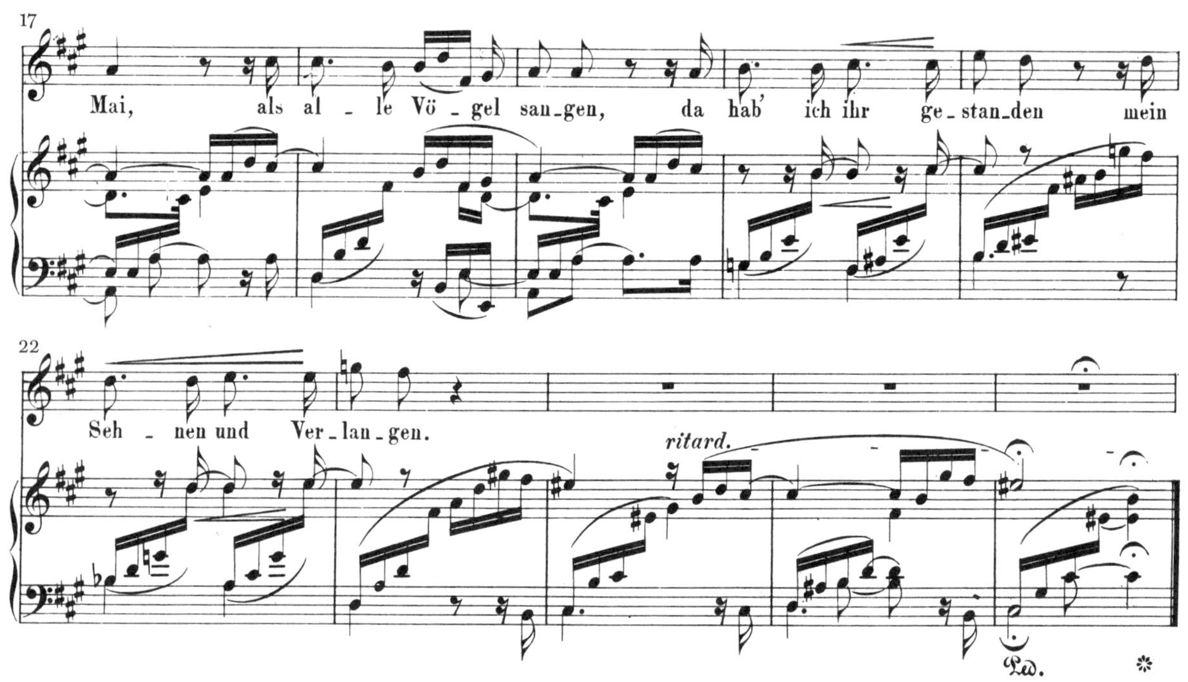


## TEXT AND TRANSLATION

"Im wunderschönen Monat Mai," from *Dichterliebe*

Im wunderschönen Monat Mai,
Als alle Knospen sprangen,
Da ist in meinem Herzen
Die Liebe aufgegangen.

Im wunderschönen Monat Mai,
Als alle Vögel sangen,
Da hab' ich ihr gestanden
Mein Sehnen und Verlangen.

"In the Lovely Month of May," from *The Poet's Love*

In the lovely month of May,
When all the buds were bursting,
Then within my heart
Love began to blossom.

In the lovely month of May,
When all the birds were singing,
Then I confessed to her
My longing and desire.

# "Ich grolle nicht"

Text by Heinrich Heine

19
f
Ich grolle nicht, und wenn das Herz auch bricht. Ich sah dich ja im
p
24
cresc.
Trau-me, und sah die Nacht in dei-nes Her - zens Rau-me, und sah die Schlang,' die dir am Her - zen
28
ritard.
frisst, ich sah, mein Lieb, wie sehr du e - lend bist. Ich grol-le nicht, ich grolle
32
nicht.

## TEXT AND TRANSLATION

"Ich grolle nicht," from *Dichterliebe*

Ich grolle nicht, und wenn das Herz auch bricht.
Ewig verlor'nes Lieb! Ich grolle nicht.
Wie du auch strahlst in Diamantenpracht,
Es fällt kein Strahl in deines Herzens Nacht.
Das weiß ich längst.

Ich grolle nicht, und wenn das Herz auch bricht.
Ich sah dich ja im Traume,
Und sah die Nacht in deines Herzens Raume,
Und sah die Schlang', die dir am Herzen frißt,
Ich sah, mein Lieb, wie sehr du elend bist.
Ich grolle nicht.

"I Bear No Grudge," from *The Poet's Love*

I bear no grudge, even if my heart breaks.
Eternally lost Love! I bear no grudge.
Even as you beam in diamond splendor,
There falls no beam into your heart's night.
That I have known for a long time.

I bear no grudge, even if my heart breaks.
I saw you in a dream,
And saw the night in the space of your heart,
And saw the snake that devours your heart;
I saw, my love, how much you are miserable.
I bear no grudge.

## Robert Schumann

"Widmung," from *Myrten,* Op. 25

Like *Dichterliebe* (p. 363), the collection of songs in *Myrten* was composed during Schumann's memorable song year, 1840. Schumann presented these songs, composed to texts by a variety of poets, to Clara as a wedding gift. This song's text is by Friedrich Rückert.

Text by Friedrich Rückert

7
le - be, mein Him - mel du, dar - ein ich schwe - be, o du mein
Ped. * Ped. * Ped. *
10
Grab, in das hin - ab ich e - wig mei - nen Kum - mer
Ped. *
13
gab! Du bist die Ruh, du
ritard.
p
3 3 3
p
16
bist der Frie - den, du bist vom

19
Him - mel mir be - schie - den. Dass du mich
22
liebst, macht mich mir werth, dein Blick hat mich vor mir ver-
25
ritard.
klärt, du hebst mich lie - bend ü - ber mich, mein
ritard.
p
28
ritard.
f
gu - ter Geist, mein bess - res Ich! Du mei - ne See - le, du mein
ritard.
f

31
Herz, du mei-ne Wonn', o du mein Schmerz, du mei-ne
34
steigend und eilend
Welt, in der ich le - be, mein Him - mel du, da - rein ich
steigend und eilend
37
ritard.
schwe - be, mein gut - er Geist, mein bess' - res Ich!
ritard.
ritard.
p
41
ritard.

## TEXT AND TRANSLATION

"Widmung," from *Myrten*

Du meine Seele, du mein Herz,
Du meine Wonn', o du mein Schmerz,
Du meine Welt, in der ich lebe,
Mein Himmel du, darein ich schwebe,
O du mein Grab, in das hinab
Ich ewig meinen Kummer gab.

Du bist die Ruh, du bist der Frieden,
Du bist der Himmel mir beschieden.
Daß du mich liebst, macht mich mir werth,
Dein Blick hat mich vor mir verklärt,
Du hebst mich liebend über mich,
Mein guter Geist, mein beßres Ich!

"Dedication," from *Myrtle*

You my soul, you my heart,
You my delight, oh you my pain,
You my world, in which I live,
My heaven you, in which I soar,
Oh you my grave, into which
I eternally pour my sorrow.

You are rest, you are peace,
You are granted to me from heaven.
That you love me makes me worthy,
Your gaze has transfigured my view of myself,
You lift me lovingly above myself,
My good spirit, my better self!

## Robert Schumann

*Papillons,* Op. 2, No. 6

This set of twelve short piano works (*Butterflies*) was published in 1831, as Schumann's Opus 2. During this time, Schumann was coping with degenerative weakness in the middle finger of his right hand, which turned him away from performance and toward literary interests. In some of his writings, he draws links between this composition and a literary inspiration: the final chapters of Jean Paul's *Flegeljahre,* which depict characters at a masked ball.

From *Piano Music of Robert Schumann, Series I.* New York: Dover Publications, Inc.

## John Philip Sousa (1854–1932)

"The Stars and Stripes Forever"

Shortly after the American bandleader John Philip Sousa composed "The Stars and Stripes Forever" for his band, the march rapidly became Sousa's most popular work: it was widely distributed in a piano score (below), played at nearly all of his concerts, and later was designated the national march of the United States. A short score excerpt is included to show the piece as a conductor would see it.

### Piano score

From *Sousa's Great Marches in Piano Transcription*. New York: Dover Publications, Inc.

28
35
1
2
ff
p
p
41
48
55
62

69
f
74
79
84
89
ff grandioso.
marcato il bassi

95
101
107
113
119
1
2

## Short score (excerpt)

11
3rd Cornet
14
17

20
1.
2.
Fl.
Cl.
p
1st and 2nd B♭ Cor.
Sop. and Alto Sax.
p-f
1-2 Cornets and Trombs. out 1st time
3 Cor. and Hns.
Bar. or Trb.
Ten. Sax.
p
p-f
(Trbe.)
Bar. and Bass Sax.
Basses
23
27

31
35
1.
2.
ff
ff
p
TRIO
Flute-Picc. 8va
Solo Cor. & Clars.
(Cl. accent 3rd beat 1st time only)
p
Bar. Alto & Ten Sax.
1-2-3 Cornets & Horns (Trpts.)
p Trbe.
Bass
38

42
(Trpts.)
46
(Trpts.)
50
p
p
B.D.

54
(Trpts.)
58
62
66

## John Philip Sousa

"The Washington Post March" (piano score)

Sousa wrote this march in 1889, when he was director of the United States Marine Band. The march, which was frequently used for dancing the two-step, was commissioned by the *Washington Post* and first performed at an awards ceremony for the newspaper's essay contest.

25
ff
31
37
1.
2.
p
41
47
53
1.
2.
ff

57
ff
63
ff
68
73
8
78
8
1.
2.

## Igor Stravinsky

"Lento," from *For the Five Fingers*

Stravinsky's *For the Five Fingers* is a collection of short teaching pieces composed in 1921. Each movement develops five-note melodies in the right hand, and only occasionally requires a change of right-hand position.

## John Tavener (b. 1944)
### "The Lamb"

Taverner composed "The Lamb" in 1982 as a birthday gift for his nephew. The text comes from William Blake's 1789 collection of poetry, *Songs of Innocence*. Though Blake set the poem to music himself, his composition has been lost.

Text by William Blake

5
poco
S
Gave thee cloth - ing of de - light, Soft - est cloth - ing, wool - ly, bright;
A
Gave thee cloth - ing of de - light, Soft - est cloth - ing, wool - ly, bright;
T
B
poco
7
Poco meno mosso
pp
S
Gave thee such a ten - der voice, Mak - ing all the vales re - joice?
pp
A
Gave thee such a ten - der voice, Mak - ing all the vales re - joice?
pp
T
Gave thee such a ten - der voice, Mak - ing all the vales re - joice?
pp
B
Gave thee such a ten - der voice, Mak - ing all the vales re - joice?
Poco meno mosso
pp

9
S
Lit-tle Lamb, who made thee? Dost thou know who made thee?
A
Lit-tle Lamb, who made thee? Dost thou know who made thee?
T
Lit-tle Lamb, who made thee? Dost thou know who made thee?
B
Lit-tle Lamb, who made thee, Dost thou know who made thee?
11
A tempo — moving forward
mp
S
Lit-tle Lamb, I'll tell thee, Lit-tle Lamb, I'll tell thee;
A
Lit-tle Lamb, I'll tell thee, Lit-tle Lamb, I'll tell thee;
T
Lit-tle Lamb, I'll tell thee, Lit-tle Lamb, I'll tell thee;
B
Lit-tle Lamb, I'll tell thee, Lit-tle Lamb, I'll tell thee;
A tempo — moving forward
mp

13
S
He is called — by thy name, For he calls him - self a Lamb.
A
He is called — by thy name, For he calls him - self a Lamb.
T
He is called — by thy name, For he calls him - self a Lamb.
B
He is called — by thy name, For he calls him - self a Lamb.
15
poco
S
He is meek, and he is mild, He be - came a lit - tle child.
A
He is meek, and he is mild, He be - came a lit - tle child.
T
He is meek, and he is mild, He be - came a lit - tle child.
B
He is meek, and he is mild, He be - came a lit - tle child.
poco

Poco meno mosso
17
pp
S
I, a child, and thou a lamb, We are called by his name.
A
I, a child, and thou a lamb, We are called by his name.
T
I, a child, and thou a lamb, We are called by his name.
B
I, a child, and thou a lamb, We are called by his name.
Poco meno mosso
19
rit.
S
Lit-tle lamb, God bless thee! Lit-tle lamb, God bless thee!
A
Lit-tle lamb, God bless thee! Lit-tle lamb, God bless thee!
T
Lit-tle lamb, God bless thee! Lit-tle lamb, God bless thee!
B
Lit-tle lamb, God bless thee! Lit-tle lamb, God bless thee!
rit.

## **Edgar Varèse (1883–1965)**

*Density 21.5,* for solo flute

The French composer Edgard Varèse wrote this piece in 1936 for the flute virtuoso Georges Barrère. The title refers to Barrère's platinum flute: the density of platinum is 21.5 grams per cubic centimeter.

Written in January 1936 at the request of Georges Barrère for the inauguration of his platinum flute. Revised April 1946. 21.5 is the density of platinum.

** Always strictly in time—follow metronomic indications.

*** Notes marked + to be played softly, hitting the keys at the same time to produce a percussive effect.

♩= 60
mp
p
mp
ff
ff
ff
♩= 72
fff
loco
♩= 60
fff
ff
p subito
f > p
f > p
f > p
♩= 72
p
p
ff
loco
♩= 60
ten.
fff
p < f > p
sfp
sfp > p
ff
p
pp
cresc. molto
ff
fff

## Anton Webern (1883–1945)

"Dies ist ein Lied," from *Fünf Lieder aus "Der siebente Ring,"* Op. 3, No. 1

Webern composed this song in 1922 as part of a collection of five songs to texts by the German poet Stefan George. George, whose poems were also set to music by Schoenberg, is considered a pivotal figure in modernist German poetry. The songs are Webern's first works that do not employ key signatures.

Text by Stefan George

9
rit.
ppp
möcht es ein Lied
das rüh - re sein.

## TEXT AND TRANSLATION

"Dies ist ein Lied," from *Fünf Lieder aus "Der siebente Ring"*

Dies ist ein Lied
Für dich allein:
Von kindischem Wähnen
Von frommen Tränen . . .
Durch Morgengärten klingt es
Ein leichtbeschwingtes.
Nur dir allein
Möcht es ein Lied
Das rühre sein.

"This Is a Song," from *Five Songs from The Seventh Ring*

This is a song
For you alone:
Of childish imagination
Of pious tears . . .
Through the morning garden it sounds
Lightly lilting.
Only for you alone
Would it like to be a song
That stirs the soul.

## Anton Webern

String Quartet, Op. 5: Third and fourth movements

These are two of five very short movements for string quartet that Webern composed in 1909, and later arranged for string orchestra. They are typical of Webern's works in that they are quite brief; indeed, all of Webern's music can fit on six compact discs.

15
tempo (𝅗𝅥 = 84)
poco a
pizz.
mf
pp
p
mp
arco
poco cresc.
poco accel.
18
f
cresc.
mp cresc.
mf
f cresc.
arco
mf cresc.
21
sehr rasch (𝅗𝅥 = 102)
ff
fff
pizz.
sfff

Sehr langsam (♪ = ca 58)
zögernd
im tempo
rit.
tempo
rit.
verklingend
tempo
rit.
tempo
mit Dämpfer
am Steg
pizz.
arco
äußerst zart
äußerst ruhig
so zart als möglich
flüchtig
ppp
pp
6
10

## Anton Webern

*Variations for Piano,* Op. 27, second movement

Webern composed this set of variations in 1935–36. In his serial works, Webern frequently made use of older forms, such as theme and variations and binary form. This movement makes unusual use of hand crossing. Try it out by sitting at a keyboard and placing your hands on the pitches designated in the score—but keeping those notated in the upper staff in your right hand, and those in the lower staff in your left.

**Meredith Willson (1902–1984)**

"Till There Was You," from *The Music Man*

This song comes from Willson's musical *The Music Man*, which opened on Broadway in 1957. In writing both the words and music, Willson drew on his Iowa childhood to tell the story of a con man, Harold Hill, who arrives in the fictitious town of River City, Iowa, to start a band, or so he claims (in reality he plans to swindle the town out of money for uniforms and instruments). He instead falls in love with the town's librarian, Marian, who sings this song. The song was included in film versions of the musical in 1962 and 2003. The Beatles recorded a version of it in 1963.

Text by Meredith Willson

10
sky, but I nev - er saw them wing - ing. No, I
13
nev - er saw them at all, till there was you.
3
16
And there was mu - sic, and there were won - der - ful
3
L.H.

19
ro - ses, they tell me, in sweet frag - rant
22
mea - dows of dawn and dew. There was
R.H.
R.H.
25
love all a - round, but I nev - er heard it
p

28
sing - ing. No, I nev - er heard it at all, till there was
31
you.
mp
mf
34
sempre cresc.

37
*f*
*cresc. molto*
L.H.
40
MARIAN:
There was love all a - round, but I
HAROLD:
There was love all a - round, but I
*ff*
*p*
43
nev - er heard it sing - ing. No, I nev - er heard it at
nev - er heard it sing - ing. No, I nev - er heard it at
3

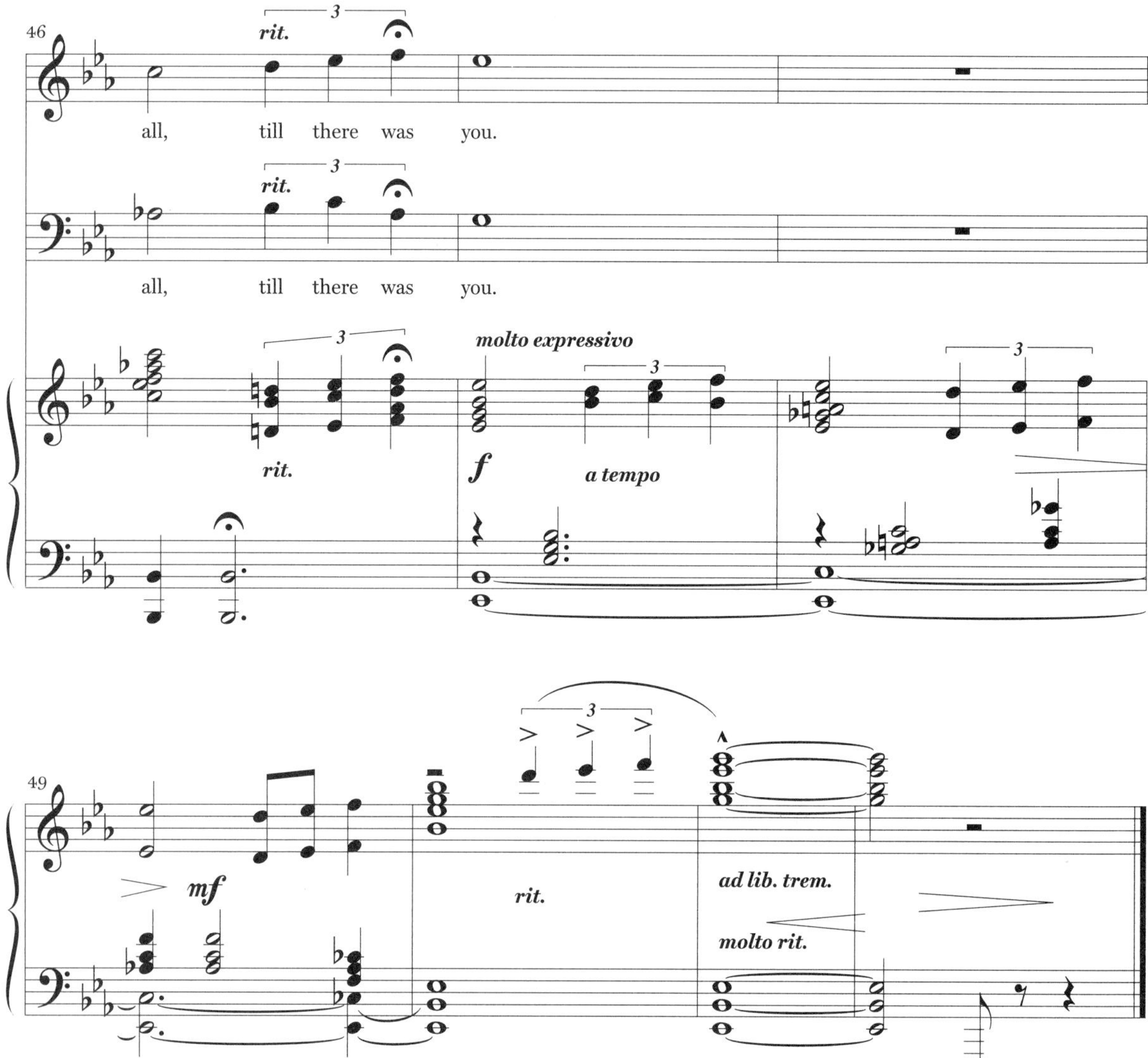
46
rit.
all, till there was you.
rit.
all, till there was you.
molto expressivo
rit.
f
a tempo
49
mf
rit.
ad lib. trem.
molto rit.

## Hugo Wolf (1860–1903)

"In dem Schatten meiner Locken," from
*Spanisches Liederbuch*

Wolf published his *Spanisches Liederbuch,* a collection of songs set to German translations of Spanish poetry, in 1891. In the late nineteenth-century, Germans were fascinated by what they considered to be the "exoticism" of Spain; consequently, Spanish poetry was popular. The text is a Renaissance poem that was also set by Brahms.

Text by Paul Heyse after Anonymous Spanish text

Leicht, zart, nicht schnell
sehr zurückhaltend
In dem Schat - ten mei-ner Lock-en schlief mir mein Ge-lieb - ter ein.
a tempo
Weck' ich ihn nun auf?
immer ppp
Ach nein!
Sorg - lich strählt' ich mei-ne krau-sen

14
Lock-en täg-lich in der Früh - e,
Doch um-sonst ist mei-ne
f
sf p
18
Mü - he, weil die Win - de sie zer - sau - sen.
sf p
sf p
f
22
p
poco rit.
3
Lock-en schat - ten, Win-des - sau - sen schlä-fer-ten den Lieb-sten
pp
pp
26
a tempo
p
ein.
Weck' ich ihn nun auf?
p
pp

30
pp
Ach nein!
f
Hö - ren muss ich, wie ihn
p
mf
35
grä - me, dass er schmach - tet schon so lan - ge, dass ihm
38
Le - ben geb' und neh - me die - se mei - ne brau - ne Wan -
mf
41
- - ge.
f
p

44
sehr zurückhaltend
p
Und er nennt mich sei - ne Schlan - ge,
und doch schlief er bei mir
47
a tempo
pp
ein.
Weck' ich ihn nun auf?
pp
immer ppp
51
Ach
nein!
55
p
dim.
pp

## TEXT AND TRANSLATION

"In dem Schatten meiner Locken," from
*Spanisches Liederbuch*

In dem Schatten meiner Locken
Schlief mir mein Geliebter ein.
Weck' ich ihn nun auf? Ach nein!

Sorglich strählt' ich meine krausen
Locken täglich in der Frühe,
Doch umsonst ist meine Mühe,
weil die Winde sie zersausen.
Lockenschatten, Windessausen
Schläferten den Liebsten ein.
Weck' ich ihn nun auf? Ach nein!

Hören muß ich, wie ihn gräme,
Daß er schmachtet schon so lange,
Daß ihm Leben geb' und nehme
Diese meine braune Wange,
Und er nennt mich eine Schlange,
Und doch schlief er bei mir ein.
Weck' ich ihn nun auf? Ach nein!

"In the shadow of my tresses," from
*Spanish Songbook*

In the shadow of my tresses
My beloved has fallen asleep.
Shall I wake him up now? Ah, no!

Carefully I comb my curly
Locks daily in the morning,
But in vain is my labor,
Because the winds tousle them.
Tress-shadows, wind-sweeping
Lulled my beloved to sleep.
Shall I wake him up now? Ah, no!

I must hear how it grieves him,
That he has languished for so long,
That life gives to him and takes from him
This, my brown cheek,
And he calls me a snake,
Yet he fell asleep by me.
Shall I wake him up now? Ah, no!

# Timeline of Works

Hymn tunes and folk songs follow at the end. Timeline headings are based on the first composition in the anthology for each composer.

## Late 17th Century:

**Archangelo Corelli (1653–1713)**

Allemanda, from Trio Sonata in A Minor, Op. 4, No. 5 (1694)
Preludio, from Sonata in D Minor, Op. 4, No. 8 (1694)

**Henry Purcell (1659–1695)**

From *Dido and Aeneas* (1689): "Ah, Belinda, I am prest," "Thy hand, Belinda" and "When I am laid in earth"
"Music for a While" (1692)

**Jeremiah Clarke (1674–1707)**

*Trumpet Voluntary (Prince of Denmark's March)* (1697–1702)

## Early 18th Century:

**Johann Sebastian Bach (1685–1750)**

Passacaglia in C Minor for organ (1708–12)
From Cantata No. 208 (*The Hunt*) (1713): "Soll denn der Pales Opfer" and "Schafe können sicher weiden"
Chaconne, from Violin Partita No. 2 in D Minor (1720)
Invention in D Minor (c. 1720)
Invention in F Major (c. 1720)
Prelude, from Cello Suite No. 2 in D Minor (c. 1720)
Fugue in D♯ Minor, from *The Well-Tempered Clavier*, Book I (1722)
Fugue in G Minor, from *The Well-Tempered Clavier*, Book I (1722)
Prelude in C Major, from *The Well-Tempered Clavier*, Book I (1722)
Prelude and Fugue in C Minor, from *The Well-Tempered Clavier*, Book I (1722)
Chorale No. 74, "O Haupt voll Blut und Wunden" (1727)
Chorale No. 1, "Aus meines Herzens Grunde" (after 1730)
Chorale No. 179, "Wachet auf" (1731)
From Cantata 140, "Wachet auf" (1731): "Er kommt"
Fugue in E♭ Major for organ (*St. Anne*) (1739)
Chorale Prelude on "Wachet auf" (1748–49)

**Anonymous**

Minuet in D Minor, from the *Anna Magdalena Bach Notebook* (c. 1725)

**George Frideric Handel (1685–1759)**

Chaconne in G Major (1733)
From *Messiah* (1741): "Rejoice greatly" and "Thy rebuke hath broken His heart"

**Domenico Scarlatti (1685–1757)**

Sonata in G Major, L. 388 (1738)

## Late 18th Century:

**Joseph Haydn (1732–1809)**

Piano Sonata No. 9 in F Major, third movement (1766)
String Quartet in D Minor, Op. 76, No. 2 (*Quinten*), Menuetto and Trio (1797)

**Muzio Clementi (1752–1832)**

Sonatina, Op. 36, No. 1, first movement (1797)

**Wolfgang Amadeus Mozart (1756–1791)**

Minuet in F Major, K. 2 (1762)
Piano Sonata in G Major, K. 283, first movement (1775)
Piano Sonata in D Major, K. 284, third movement (1775)
*Variations on "Ah, vous dirai-je Maman"* (1781–82)
String Quartet in D Minor, K. 421, first and third movements (1783)
From *The Marriage of Figaro* (1786): "Quanto duolmi, Susanna" and "Voi, che sapete"
Piano Sonata in C Major, K. 545 (1788)
From *Requiem* (1791): Kyrie eleison (excerpt) and Dies irae

**Ludwig van Beethoven (1770–1827)**

Sonatina in F Major, Op. Posth., second movement (c. 1790–92)
Piano Sonata in C Minor, Op. 13 (*Pathétique*), second and third movements (1799)
Piano Sonata in C Major, Op. 53 (*Waldstein*), first movement (1805)
*Für Elise* (1810)

## Early 19th Century:

**Franz Schubert (1797–1828)**

"Erlkönig" (1815)
Waltz in B Minor, D. 145, No. 6 (1815)
"Du bist die Ruh" (1823)
From *Die schöne Müllerin* (1823): "Der Neugierige" and "Morgengruss"
"Der Lindenbaum," from *Winterreise* (1828)
From *Moments musicaux*, Op. 94: No 6, in A♭ Major (1828)

**Fanny Mendelssohn Hensel (1805–1847)**

"Neue Liebe, neues Leben" (1836)
"Bitte" (published 1848)
"Nachtwanderer" (published 1848)

**Frédéric Chopin (1810–1849)**

Nocturne in E♭ Major, Op. 9, No. 2 (1832)
Prelude in C Minor, Op. 28, No. 20 (1839)
Mazurka in F Minor, Op. 68, No. 4 (1846)

**Robert Schumann (1810–1856)**
*Papillons*, Op. 2, No. 6 (1831)
From *Dichterliebe* (1840): "Im wunderschönen Monat Mai" and "Ich grolle nicht"
"Widmung," from *Myrten*, Op. 25 (1840)
From *Album for the Young*, Op. 68 (1848): No. 3: "Trällerliedchen" and No. 8: "Wilder Reiter"

**Clara Schumann (1819–1896)**
"Liebst du um Schönheit" (1841)

## Late 19th Century:

**Johannes Brahms (1833–1897)**
"Die Mainacht" (1866)
*Variations on a Theme by Haydn*, theme (1873)
Intermezzo in A Major, Op. 118, No. 2 (1893)

**Gabriel Fauré (1845–1924)**
"Après un rêve" (1877)

**John Philip Sousa (1854–1932)**
"The Washington Post March" (1889)
"The Stars and Stripes Forever" (1897)

**Hugo Wolf (1860–1903)**
"In dem Schatten meiner Locken," from *Spanisches Liederbuch* (1891)

## Early 20th Century:

**Claude Debussy (1862–1918)**
"La cathédrale engloutie," from *Préludes* (1910)

**Scott Joplin (c. 1867–1917)**
"Pine Apple Rag" (1908)
"Solace" (1909)

**Arnold Schoenberg (1874–1951)**
*Klavierstück*, Op. 33a (1929)

**Maurice Ravel (1875–1937)**
"Aoua!," from *Chansons madécasses*, for flute, cello, piano, and soprano (1925–26)

**Béla Bartók (1881–1945)**
*Bagatelle*, Op. 6, No. 2 (1908)
"Song of the Harvest," for two violins (1931)
"Bulgarian Rhythm," from *Mikrokosmos* (No. 115) (1940)
"From the Isle of Bali," from *Mikrokosmos* (No. 109) (1940)

**Igor Stravinsky (1882–1971)**
"Lento," from *For the Five Fingers* (1921)

**Anton Webern (1883–1945)**
"Dies ist ein Lied," from *Fünf Lieder aus "Der siebente Ring,"* Op. 3, No. 1 (1909)
String Quartet, Op. 5, third and fourth movements (1909)
*Symphonie*, Op. 21, second movement (1929)
*Variations for Piano*, Op. 27, second movement (1935–36)

**Edgard Varèse (1883–1965)**
*Density 21.5*, for solo flute (1936)

**George Gershwin (1898–1937)**
"'S Wonderful!" (1927)
"I Got Rhythm" (1930)

## Late 20th Century:

**Meredith Willson (1902–1984)**
"Till There Was You," from *The Music Man* (1957)

**Luigi Dallapiccola (1904–1975)**
"Die Sonne kommt," from *Goethe-lieder*, for voice and clarinets (1953)

**Samuel Barber (1910–1981)**
"Sea-Snatch," from *Hermit Songs* (1952–53)

**John Barnes Chance (1932–1972)**
*Variations on a Korean Folk Song*, excerpts (1967)

**Krzysztof Penderecki (b. 1933)**
*Threnody for the Victims of Hiroshima* (to rehearsal 25) (1960)

**Steve Reich (b. 1936)**
*Piano Phase* (patterns 1–32) (1967)

**John Corigliano (b. 1938)**
"Come now, my darling," from *The Ghosts of Versailles* (1987)

**John Tavener (b. 1944)**
"The Lamb" (1982)

---

**Hymn Tunes**
"Chartres" (15th century French melody, harmonization by Charles Wood)
"Old Hundredth" (harmonization by Louis Bourgeois, 1551)
"Rosa Mystica" (traditional melody, harmonization by Michael Praetorius, 1609)
"St. Anne Chorale" (William Croft, 1708)
"America" (Thesaurus Musicus, 1740)
"St. George's Windsor" (harmonization by George J. Elvey, 1858)

**Folk Songs**
"Greensleeves" (English tune, first referenced 1580)
"Down in the Valley" (American folk tune, first printed c. 1910)

# DVD Contents and Performers

**Anonymous**
Minuet in D Minor, from the *Anna Magdalena Bach Notebook*
William Porter, harpsichord

**Johann Sebastian Bach**
From Cantata No. 140, "Wachet auf": "Er kommt" (recitative)
Robert Swensen, tenor; Richard Masters, harpsichord

From Cantata No. 208 (*The Hunt*): "Soll denn der Pales Opfer" (recitative) and "Schafe können sicher weiden" (aria)
Andrea Folan, soprano; Sophia Gibbs Kim and Carmen Lemoine, flutes; Kathleen Murphy Kemp, cello; Richard Masters, harpsichord

Chaconne, from Violin Partita No. 2 in D Minor
Oleh Krysa, violin

Chorale: "Aus meines Herzens Grunde" (No. 1) (choir)
Third Presbyterian Church Choir (Rochester, NY); Peter DuBois, conductor

Chorale: "Aus meines Herzens Grunde" (No. 1) (organ, soprano-bass)
Peter DuBois, organ

Chorale: "Aus meines Herzens Grunde" (No. 1) (organ, SATB)
Peter DuBois, organ

Chorale: "O Haupt voll Blut und Wunden" (No. 74) (choir)
Third Presbyterian Church Choir (Rochester, NY); Peter DuBois, conductor

Chorale: "O Haupt voll Blut und Wunden" (No. 74) (organ, soprano-bass)
Peter DuBois, organ

Chorale: "O Haupt voll Blut und Wunden" (No. 74) (organ, SATB)
Peter DuBois, organ

Chorale: "Wachet auf" (No. 179) (choir)
Third Presbyterian Church Choir (Rochester, NY); Peter DuBois, conductor

Chorale: "Wachet auf" (No. 179) (organ, soprano-bass)
Peter DuBois, organ

Chorale: "Wachet auf" (No. 179) (organ, SATB)
Peter DuBois, organ

Chorale Prelude on "Wachet auf" (Schübler Chorale)
Peter DuBois, organ

Invention in D Minor (harpsichord)
William Porter, harpsichord

Invention in D Minor (piano)
Sarah Rhee, piano

Invention in F Major
Howard Spindler, piano

Fugue in E♭ Major for organ (*St. Anne*), from *Clavierübung* III
Peter DuBois, organ

Passacaglia in C Minor for organ
Peter DuBois, organ

Prelude, from Cello Suite No. 2 in D Minor
Kathleen Murphy Kemp, cello

From *The Well-Tempered Clavier*, Book I: Prelude in C Major (harpsichord)
William Porter, harpsichord

From *The Well-Tempered Clavier*, Book I: Prelude in C Major (piano)
Sarah Rhee, piano

From *The Well-Tempered Clavier*, Book I: Prelude in C Minor
Howard Spindler, piano

From *The Well-Tempered Clavier*, Book I: Fugue in C Minor
Howard Spindler, piano

From *The Well-Tempered Clavier*, Book I: Fugue in D♯ Minor
Anna Maimine, piano

From *The Well-Tempered Clavier*, Book I: Fugue in G Minor
Anna Maimine, piano

**Samuel Barber**
"Sea-Snatch," from *Hermit Songs*
Kimberly Upcraft-Russ, soprano; Richard Masters, piano

**Béla Bartók**
*Bagatelle*, Op. 6, No. 2
Robert Wason, piano

From *Mikrokosmos:* "Bulgarian Rhythm" (No. 115)
Robert Wason, piano

From *Mikrokosmos:* "From the Isle of Bali" (No. 109)
Anna Maimine, piano

"Song of the Harvest," for two violins
Timothy Ying and Janet Ying, violins

**Ludwig van Beethoven**
*Für Elise*
Richard Masters, piano

Piano Sonata in C Minor, Op. 13 (*Pathétique*), second movement
Kristian Bezuidenhout, fortepiano

Piano Sonata in C Minor, Op. 13 (*Pathétique*), third movement
Sergio Monteiro, piano

Piano Sonata in C Major, Op. 53 (*Waldstein*), first movement
Sergio Monteiro, piano

Sonatina in F Major, Op. Posth., second movement
Sergio Monteiro, piano

**Johannes Brahms**
"Die Mainacht"
Robert Swensen, tenor; Richard Masters, piano

Intermezzo in A Major, Op. 118, No. 2
Sarah Rhee, piano

*Variations on a Theme by Haydn,* theme (two pianos)
Anna Maimine and Richard Masters, pianos

**John Barnes Chance**
*Variations on a Korean Folk Song,* mm. 1–52
Tokyo Kosei Wind Orchestra; Frederick Fennell, conductor

*Variations on a Korean Folk Song,* mm. 199–214
Tokyo Kosei Wind Orchestra; Frederick Fennell, conductor

**Frédéric Chopin**
Mazurka in F Minor, Op. 68, No. 4
Anna Maimine, piano

Nocturne in E♭ Major, Op. 9, No. 2
Sarah Rhee, piano

Prelude in C Minor, Op. 28, No. 20
Sarah Rhee, piano

**Jeremiah Clarke**
*Trumpet Voluntary (Prince of Denmark's March)*
Douglas Prosser, trumpet; Peter DuBois, organ

**Muzio Clementi**
Sonatina, Op. 36, No. 1, first movement
Sergio Monteiro, piano

**Archangelo Corelli**
Allemanda, from Trio Sonata in A Minor, Op. 4, No. 5
Timothy Ying and Janet Ying, violins; David Ying, cello; William Porter, harpsichord

Preludio, from Sonata in D Minor, Op. 4, No. 8
Margaret Leenhouts and Megan Kemp, violins; Kathleen Murphy Kemp, cello; Richard Masters, harpsichord

**John Corigliano**
"Come Now, My Darling," from *The Ghosts of Versailles*
Elizabeth W. Marvin, soprano; Kathryn Cowdrick, mezzo-soprano; Jean Barr, piano

**Luigi Dallapiccola**
"Die Sonne kommt," from *Goethe-lieder,* for voice and clarinets
Heather Gardner, soprano; Juliet Grabowski, clarinet

**Claude Debussy**
"La cathédrale engloutie," from *Préludes*
Anna Maimine, piano

**"Down in the Valley,"** arr. Norman Lloyd
Kimberly Upcraft-Russ, soprano; Richard Masters, piano

**Gabriel Fauré**
"Après un rêve"
Robert Swensen, tenor; Richard Masters, piano

**Stephen Foster**
"Jeanie with the Light Brown Hair," arr. Norman Lloyd
Robert Swensen, tenor; Richard Masters, piano

**George Gershwin**
"I Got Rhythm," from *Girl Crazy*
Elizabeth W. Marvin, soprano; Robert Wason, piano

"'S Wonderful!," from *Funny Face*
Robert Swensen, tenor; Kathryn Cowdrick, mezzo-soprano; Robert Wason, piano

**"Greensleeves,"** arr. John Duarte; arr. Norbert Kraft
Petar Kodzas, guitar

**George Frideric Handel**
Chaconne in G Major
William Porter, harpsichord

From *Messiah:* "Rejoice greatly"
Elizabeth W. Marvin, soprano; Peter DuBois, organ

From *Messiah:* "Thy rebuke hath broken His heart"
Robert Swensen, tenor; Richard Masters, harpsichord

**Joseph Haydn**
Piano Sonata No. 9 in F Major, third movement (fortepiano)
Kristian Bezuidenhout, fortepiano

Piano Sonata No. 9 in F Major, third movement (piano)
Howard Spindler, piano

String Quartet in D Minor, Op. 76, No. 2 (*Quinten*), Minuetto and Trio
J. Bang and Quizhen Liu, violins; Jiazhi Wang, viola; Xinyi Xu, cello

**Fanny Mendelssohn Hensel**
"Bitte," Op. 7, No. 5
Allyn Van Dusen, mezzo-soprano; Howard Spindler, piano

"Nachtwanderer," Op. 7, No. 1
Allyn Van Dusen, mezzo-soprano; Howard Spindler, piano

"Neue Liebe, neues Leben"
Robert Swensen, tenor; Russell Miller, piano

**Hymn tunes**
"America" ("My Country, 'Tis of Thee") (choir)
Third Presbyterian Church Choir (Rochester, NY); Peter DuBois, conductor

"America" ("My Country, 'Tis of Thee") (organ, soprano-bass)
Peter DuBois, organ

"America" ("My Country, 'Tis of Thee") (organ, SATB)
Peter DuBois, organ

"Chartres" (organ, soprano-bass)
Peter DuBois, organ

"Chartres" (organ, SATB)
Peter DuBois, organ

"Old Hundredth" (organ, soprano-bass)
Peter DuBois, organ

"Old Hundredth" (organ, SATB)
Peter DuBois, organ

"Rosa Mystica" (organ, soprano-bass)
Peter DuBois, organ

"Rosa Mystica" (organ, SATB)
Peter DuBois, organ

"St. Anne Chorale" (organ, soprano-bass)
Peter DuBois, organ

"St. Anne Chorale" (organ, SATB)
Peter DuBois, organ

"St. George's Windsor" (organ, soprano-bass)
Peter DuBois, organ

"St. George's Windsor" (organ, SATB)
Peter DuBois, organ

**Scott Joplin**

"Pine Apple Rag"
Tony Caramia, piano

"Solace"
Tony Caramia, piano

"Solace" (with improvisation)
Tony Caramia, piano

**Wolfgang Amadeus Mozart**

From *The Marriage of Figaro:* "Quanto duolmi, Susanna" (recitative)
Seyoung Jeong and Julie Allison Norman, sopranos; Abigail Levis, mezzo-soprano; Eastman Opera Theater Orchestra; Benton Hess, conductor

From *The Marriage of Figaro:* "Voi che sapete" (aria)
Abigail Levis, mezzo-soprano; Eastman Opera Theater Orchestra; Benton Hess, conductor

Minuet in F Major, K. 2
Howard Spindler, piano

Piano Sonata in G Major, K. 283, first movement
Kristian Bezuidenhout, fortepiano

Piano Sonata in D Major, K. 284, third movement
Kristian Bezuidenhout, fortepiano

Piano Sonata in C Major, K. 545
Kristian Bezuidenhout, fortepiano
first movement
second movement
third movement

Piano Sonata in C Major, K. 545
Howard Spindler, piano
first movement
second movement
third movement

From *Requiem*: Kyrie eleison
Eastman Philharmonia, Eastman Chorale, and Eastman-Rochester Chorus; Shinik Ham, conductor

From *Requiem*: Dies irae
Eastman Philharmonia, Eastman Chorale, and Eastman-Rochester Chorus; Shinik Ham, conductor

String Quartet in D Minor, K. 421, first movement
J. Bang and Quizhen Liu, violins; Jiazhi Wang, viola; Xinyi Xu, cello

String Quartet in D Minor, K. 421, third movement
Ying Quartet

*Variations on "Ah, vous dirai-je Maman"*
Sergio Monteiro, piano

**Krzysztof Penderecki**

*Threnody for the Victims of Hiroshima* (to rehearsal 25)
Eastman Philharmonia; Bradley Lubman, conductor

**Henry Purcell**

From *Dido and Aeneas:* "Ah, Belinda, I am prest"
Andrea Folan, soprano; Kathleen Murphy Kemp, cello; Richard Masters, piano

From *Dido and Aeneas:* "Thy hand, Belinda" and "When I am laid in earth"
Andrea Folan, soprano; Kathleen Murphy Kemp, cello; Richard Masters, piano

"Music for a While" (soprano with piano accompaniment)
Kimberly Upcraft-Russ, soprano; Richard Masters, piano

"Music for a While" (soprano with continuo accompaniment)
Elizabeth W. Marvin, soprano; David Ying, cello; William Porter, harpischord

**Maurice Ravel**

"Aoua!," from *Chansons madécasses,* for flute, cello, piano, and soprano
Yvonne Douthat, mezzo-soprano; Sean Owen, flute; James Kim, cello; Joo Hyun Lee, piano

**Steve Reich**

*Piano Phase* (patterns 1–32)
Winnie Cheung and David Plylar, pianos

**Domenico Scarlatti**

Sonata in G Major, L. 388
Anna Maimine, piano

**Arnold Schoenberg**

*Klavierstück,* Op. 33a
Thomas Rosenkranz, piano

**Franz Schubert**

From *Die schöne Müllerin:* "Der Neugierige"
Robert Swensen, tenor; Richard Masters, piano

From *Die schöne Müllerin:* "Morgengruß"
Robert Swensen, tenor; Richard Masters, piano

"Du bist die Ruh"
Robert Swensen, tenor; Richard Masters, piano

"Erlkönig"
Robert Swensen, tenor; Russell Miller, piano

From *Moments musicaux,* Op. 94: No. 6 in A♭ Major
Anna Maimine, piano

Waltz in B Minor, D. 145, No. 6
Robert Wason, piano

"Der Lindenbaum," from *Winterreise*
Robert Swensen, tenor; Russell Miller, piano

**Clara Schumann**
"Liebst du um Schönheit"
Elizabeth W. Marvin, soprano; Jean Barr, piano

**Robert Schumann**
From *Album for the Young,* Op. 68: No. 3: "Trällerliedchen"
Sergio Monteiro, piano

From *Album for the Young,* Op. 68: No. 8: "Wilder Reiter"
Sarah Rhee, piano

From *Dichterliebe:* "Im wunderschönen Monat Mai"
Robert Swensen, tenor; Paula Fan, piano

From *Dichterliebe:* "Ich grolle nicht"
Robert Swensen, tenor; Paula Fan, piano

"Widmung," from *Myrten,* Op. 25
Allyn Van Dusen, mezzo-soprano; Howard Spindler, piano

*Papillons,* Op. 2, No. 6
Richard Masters, piano

**John Philip Sousa**
"The Stars and Stripes Forever"
Eastman Wind Ensemble; Donald Hunsberger, conductor

"The Washington Post March" (band)
Eastman Wind Ensemble; Donald Hunsberger, conductor

"The Washington Post March" (piano)
Richard Masters, piano

**Igor Stravinsky**
"Lento," from *For the Five Fingers*
Sergio Monteiro, piano

**John Tavener**
"The Lamb"
Third Presbyterian Church Choir (Rochester, NY); Peter DuBois, conductor

**Edgard Varèse**
*Density 21.5,* for solo flute
Sophia Gibbs Kim, flute

**Anton Webern**
"Dies ist ein Lied," from *Fünf Lieder aus "Der siebente Ring,"* Op. 3, No. 1
Katherine Maroney, mezzo-soprano; Christina Yue, piano

String Quartet, Op. 5, third movement
Ying Quartet

String Quartet, Op. 5, fourth movement
Ying Quartet

*Variations for Piano,* Op. 27, second movement
Robert Wason, piano

**Meredith Willson**
"Till There Was You," from *The Music Man*
Kimberly Upcraft-Russ, soprano; Evan Jones, baritone; Richard Masters, piano

**Hugo Wolf**
"In dem Schatten meiner Locken," from *Spanisches Liederbuch*
Kimberly Upcraft-Russ, soprano; Richard Masters, piano